for 3 - 9s

Book 4

CHRISTIAN FOCUS PUBLICATIONS

We believe that the Bible is God's word to mankind, and that it contains everything we need to know in order to be reconciled with God and live in a way that is pleasing to him. Therefore, we believe it is vital to teach children accurately from the Bible, being careful to teach each passage's true meaning in an appropriate way for children, rather than selecting a 'children's message' from a Biblical passage.

© TnT Ministries
29 Buxton Gardens, Acton, London, W3 9LE
Tel: (0181) 992 0450

Published in 1998 by Christian Focus Publications Ltd.
Geanies House, Fearn, Tain, Ross-shire, IV20 1TW
Tel: (01862) 871 011 Fax: (01862) 871 699

Cover design by Douglas McConnach

Production by Shadbolt Associates. Tel +44 (0)181 325 3131

This book and others in the series can be purchased from
your local Christian bookshop. Alternatively you can write to
TnT Ministries direct or place your order with the publisher.

ISBN 1-85792-324-3

TnT Ministries (which stands for Teaching and Training) was launched in February 1993 by Christians from a broad variety of denominational backgrounds who were concerned that teaching the Bible to children should be taken seriously. They have been in charge of the Sunday School of 50 teachers at St Helen's Bishopsgate, an evangelical church in the City of London, for 13 years, during which time a range of Biblical teaching materials has been developed. TnT Ministries also runs training days for Sunday School teachers.

CONTENTS
On the Way for 3-9s / Book 4

Preparation of Bible material:
Thalia Blundell, David & Christine James

Editing:
David Jackman

Illustrations:
Ben Desmond

Craft Activities:
Lynda Beckett, Thalia Blundell, Sue Chapman, Annie Gemmill, Ian Masters, Kathy Pierce, Andrew Blundell

On the Way works on a three year syllabus. It covers the main Bible stories from Genesis to the Acts of the Apostles. All the Bible stories are taught as truth and not myth.

Each year the birth of Jesus is taught at Christmas, and the death and resurrection of Jesus at Easter. Between Christmas and Easter the syllabus covers aspects of Jesus' life and teaching, and after Easter there is a short series on the Early Church. The rest of the year is spent looking at the Old Testament stories, covering broad sweeps of Old Testament history. In this way leaders and children gain an orderly and cohesive view of God's dealings with his people throughout the Old and New Testaments.

The lessons are grouped in series, each of which is introduced by a series overview stating the aims of the series, the lesson aim for each week and an appropriate memory verse.

Every lesson, in addition to a lesson aim, has Bible study notes to enable the teacher to understand the passage, suggestions for visual aids and an activity for the children to take home. One activity is suitable for 3-5 year olds, one for 5-7 year olds and one for 7-9s.

How to Prepare a Lesson

To prepare a Sunday School lesson properly takes at least one evening (2-3 hours). It is helpful to read the Bible passage several days before teaching it to allow time to mull over what it is saying.

When preparing a lesson the following steps should be taken -

1. PRAY!

In a busy world this is very easy to forget. We are unable to understand God's word without his help and we need to remind ourselves of that fact before we start.

2. READ THE BIBLE PASSAGE

This should be done **before** reading the lesson manual. Our resource is the Bible, not what someone says about it. The Bible study notes in the lesson manual are a commentary on the passage to help you understand it.

3. LOOK AT THE LESSON AIM

This should reflect the main teaching of the passage. Plan how that can be packaged appropriately for the age group you teach.

4. STORYTELLING

Decide how to tell the Bible story. Is it appropriate to recapitulate on what has happened in previous weeks? Will you involve the children in the presentation of the story? What sort of questions are appropriate to use? How will you ascertain what has been understood? Is there anything in the story that should be applied to their lives?

5. VISUAL AIDS

What type of visual aid will help bring the story alive for the children? Simple pictures may be appropriate. For stories with a lot of movement it may be better to use flannelgraphs or suedegraphs. In some instances models may be appropriate, e.g. the paralysed man being let down through a hole in the roof. Do remember that visual aids take time to make and this will need to be built into your lesson preparation.

6. CRAFT ACTIVITIES

Many of the craft activities require prior preparation by the teacher so do not leave it until the night before!

Benefits of On the Way

- Encourages the leaders to study the Bible for themselves.
- Chronological approach gives leaders and children a proper view of God's dealings with his people.
- Each lesson has 3 age related craft activities.
- Everything you need is in the one book, so there is no need to buy children's activity books.
- Undated materials allow you to use the lessons to fit your situation without wasting materials.
- Once you have the entire syllabus, there is no need to repurchase.

Teacher's Challenge

Located throughout this book are cartoons highlighting some aspects of the Bible passages. Hidden in one or more of these cartoons is a bookworm (see box on right - not actual size).

If you consider yourself observant and want a challenge, count the number of times the bookworm appears in this edition. The correct answer is on the back page. Don't look until you are sure you have found them all!

Joseph

Overview

Week 1	HATED BY HIS BROTHERS To discover what happens when family relationships go wrong.	*Genesis 37:1-36*
Week 2	IMPRISONED IN EGYPT To teach that God was with Joseph in every situation.	*Genesis 39:1 - 40:23*
Week 3	GIVEN HIGH OFFICE To show how God gets Joseph into a position where he can save God's people.	*Genesis 41:1-57*
Week 4	RECONCILED WITH HIS BROTHERS To see the fulfilment of God's plan for Joseph.	*Genesis 42:1 - 46:7*

Series Aims

1. To understand the stories in their context.

2. To see how God uses a seemingly impossible situation to further his purposes for his people.

The story of Joseph is a graphic picture of God's sovereignty and demonstrates how God is able to use a seemingly impossible situation to further his own purposes.

Joseph was the eleventh son of Jacob and first son of Rachel (Genesis 30:22-24). As a result he was Jacob's favourite (Genesis 37:3). This favouritism led to family disharmony, the brothers becoming so jealous that they hated Joseph and 'could not speak to him in a friendly manner' (Genesis 37:4). Eventually the brothers seized their chance and sold Joseph into slavery in Egypt.

Whilst in Egypt Joseph was unjustly imprisoned, but through all this we are told that God was with him (Genesis 39:2,21,23). After 2 years, through his God-given ability to interpret dreams (Genesis 41:37-41),

Joseph was brought to the notice of the king of Egypt. Joseph's wisdom commended him to the king (Genesis 41:37-41) and Joseph was made Governor of all Egypt. In this position he was able to so order the affairs of Egypt during the 7 years of plenty that, when the 7 years of famine came, Egypt, the surrounding countries, and Joseph's own family were saved from starvation. The story ends with Joseph becoming reconciled to his brothers, followed by his whole family settling in Goshen in the land of Egypt.

Eventually Jacob died and was buried. Then Joseph's brothers came to him to ask forgiveness for what they had done to him in his youth. Joseph reassured his brothers by pointing out that, although they meant it for evil, God meant it for good (Genesis 50:20).

Memory work

The Lord will hear when I call to him.
Psalm 4:3

WEEK 1
Hated By His Brothers

Preparation:
Read Genesis 37:1 - 36, using the
Bible study notes to help you.

Lesson Aim:
To discover what happens when family
relationships go wrong.

In returning to Canaan to be with his father, Isaac, Jacob had faced the anger of Laban (Genesis 31:26) and the fear of revenge by his brother Esau, but through all this he was aware of God's presence in his life (Genesis 31:5-7). God was protecting and blessing him, fulfilling the promises he had made to Abraham (Genesis 12:7; 35:9-12).

In the years following his return to Canaan Jacob moved around from Succoth to Shechem to Bethel, etc. Rachel died giving birth to the last of his twelve sons, Benjamin (Genesis 35:18) and Jacob and Esau came together again at the deathbed of Isaac (Genesis 35:29). Family relationships within Jacob's household were strained. Joseph was becoming an increasing irritant to his brothers, doing nothing to play down the favouritism his father showed towards him. He probably saw it as his duty to report the slothful service of his four half brothers to his father (Genesis 37:2), but his action only increased their resentment.

The brothers appear to be morally undisciplined, immature and cynical (see also Genesis 35:22), whereas Joseph is portrayed as being spiritually aware yet needing to learn humility and wisdom in the ways of the world. Jacob had learned nothing from his own early experience of favouritism. Yet, from these tensions of a family in crisis, God was to forge a nation set apart for his own purposes, in fulfilment of his promise to Abraham.

37:2   Joseph was the eleventh son of Jacob but the first-born of Rachel, the wife Jacob had loved (35:24). Joseph's brothers, the sons of the 2 maidservants, were probably sensitive about their position, bearing in mind what had happened to Ishmael, the son of Sarah's maidservant Hagar (Genesis 21:19-21).

37:3   A tunic with long sleeves indicated the status of the wearer. He was not expected to do manual work - the long sleeves would have got in the way. It was a sign that Joseph, the first-born of the favoured wife, was Jacob's heir, even though he was younger than 10 of his brothers.

37:4   Favouritism led to jealousy and hatred.

37:10   Jacob took offence, not knowing that Joseph's dominion over him would operate within the context of the family's sojourn in Egypt and would not involve any usurping of his patriarchal authority.

37:10   'Your mother' - Rachel was already dead (35:19), so this probably referred to Leah.

37:11   Jacob's experience of God had taught him to allow for God's hand in affairs and for his right choice among men. See also

Mary's response in Luke 2:51.

37:12   Shechem was approximately one day's journey from Hebron.

37:15-17   Joseph was concerned about proper obedience. His brothers were not where they should have been, so he could have returned home and reported to his father. Instead he looked for them.

37:18-20   Hatred led to attempted murder.

37:21   Reuben was the eldest son and thus responsible for his brother's welfare.

37:25   Ishmaelites were the descendants of Ishmael. The term is interchangeable with Midianites in this context (v.28). The Midianites were also descended from Abraham (25:1-6). They inhabited desert areas east of the River Jordan and were traders.

37:28   Twenty pieces of silver was the going rate for a slave.

37:29   Reuben was absent while this was going on.

37:31-32   The lie is implied, even though it is not spoken.

37:34   Sackcloth was made from goats' hair and was very irritant. It was worn as a sign of mourning.

37:35   Jacob's reaction showed how disjointed family relationships had become; all his other children were no comfort compared to the loss of his beloved son, Joseph.

Lesson Plan

This is the first lesson in the series on Joseph. Start by asking the children who has any brothers or sisters. Ask them how many brothers and sisters they have. See who has the most. Today's true story from the Bible is about a boy with 11 brothers and 1 sister. His name was Joseph and he was 17 years old. That's the same age as .... (specify someone they know). Ask the children if they would like as many brothers and sisters as that. Ask them if they always get on with their brothers/sisters. What happens when the brother/sister annoys them? Today we will find out what happened to Joseph when he annoyed his brothers.

At the end of the story discuss with the children the problems that occurred in Joseph's family - how favouritism led to envy, anger, hatred, getting rid of Joseph. Even though Joseph had contributed to his problems the punishment meted out by his brothers was wrong.

Teach the memory verse. Ask the children if they think Joseph would have believed that God heard him. Point out that God always keeps his word. (The older children may remember other Bible characters who discovered that, e.g. Abraham.) So even when God does not appear to have heard us, we can be confident that he has. Next week we will see how God helped Joseph.

Visual Aids

For a large group use pictures or flannelgraph. You need Jacob, the 10 older brothers, Benjamin, 1 sister, some sheep, the 2 dreams.

For a smaller group use models with a pit to drop Joseph into. Either glue pictures onto card with a flat base and back support (see diagram) or make yoghurt pot people. An ice-cream container makes a good pit.

For yoghurt pot people you need yoghurt pots or plastic drinking cups, egg cartons, scraps of material, wool, rubber bands, cotton wool, sellotape, glue, pens. Cut the head from an egg carton and sellotape onto a yoghurt pot or plastic cup. Draw on a face. Dress with a piece of material secured round the middle with wool or a rubber band. Tuck the bottom edge of the material inside the bottom of the pot. Attach the head-dress in similar fashion to the robe. Glue on cotton wool as a beard if required.

Activities / 3 - 5s

Photocopy page 9 on paper and page 10 on card for each child. Prior to the lesson make up the story box according to the instructions on the page. Cut out the 4 pictures and place in an envelope for each child. The children colour the pictures and glue them round the box in the order of the story.

Activities / 5 - 7s

Make a model of Joseph in the pit. Each child requires page 11 photocopied on card, 1 toilet roll tube or half a paper towel tube, 1 garden stick approximately 30 cm long, and a piece of material 20 x 15 cm. Also required are sellotape, glue, a needle and thread.

Prior to the lesson cut out the figure of Joseph and the memory verse rectangle from page 11. Using a needle and thread, gather up one long edge of the piece of material.

Instructions
1. Colour Joseph and fold in half.
2. Glue the 2 sides of Joseph together with the garden stick in the middle. The top of the garden stick is at the top of Joseph's head.

3. Take the piece of material, gather up the prepared edge and tie tightly around Joseph's ankles.
4. Place the stick through the middle of the cardboard tube with Joseph at the top. Using sellotape fix the lower edge of the material around the top of the cardboard tube (see diagram).

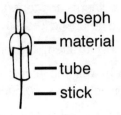

5. Glue the memory verse around the outside of the tube.
6. Joseph can be pulled into the pit and pushed out again.

Activities / 7 - 9s

Photocopy page 12 for each child. Do the puzzle as a group, then discuss the question at the bottom of the page.

Joseph was Jacob's favourite son.

Joseph's 10 brothers hated him.

Joseph dreamed that his father, mother and 11 brothers would bow down to him.

Joseph's 10 brothers put him in a pit, then sold him as a slave.

side 4

1. Cut out, score and fold along dotted lines.

2. Glue side 4 to the remaining 3 sides.

3. Glue the top flaps inside the sides to make a box open at the bottom.

The Lord will hear when I call to him.

Psalm 4:3

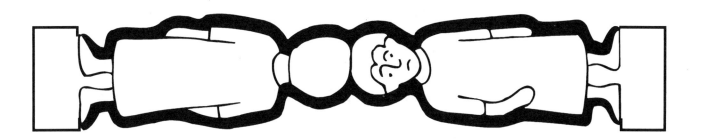

The Lord will hear

when I call to him.

Psalm 4:3

Use the following code to work out your memory verse.

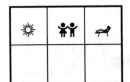	⊕	➤	🚂	🛋	🧸	🚪	👫	🚿	🪜	⛴	🚋	🌐
a	b	c	d	e	f	g	h	i	j	k	l	m

🎁	🎣	🌧	☁	❄	☁	☀	☁	☀	🧳	⚽	🧹	🚲
n	o	p	q	r	s	t	u	v	w	x	y	z

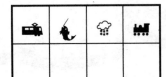

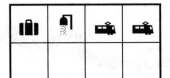

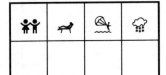

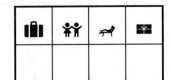

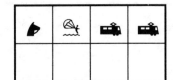

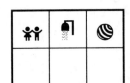

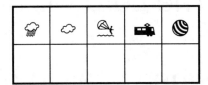

4:3

Think of situations where favouritism can occur.

How does favouritism affect the way people get on together?

Preparation:
Read Genesis 39:1 - 40:23, using the Bible study notes to help you.

39:2   Joseph had gone from being the favoured son and heir to being a slave, but God was still with him.

39:3-6   Joseph became a trusted slave of Potiphar and was appointed overseer of his house. The blessings that Potiphar's household received are an example of the overflow of God's covenant blessings. See also Jacob and Laban (30:27).

39:6b-7,10   Joseph's temptation was constant and unremitting.

39:9   Joseph recognised that all sin is against God (see also Psalm 51:4).

39:10   Joseph not only said, 'No', but also avoided the temptation whenever possible.

39:11-18   Joseph found himself in a no-win situation (v.14), because of the unsatisfied pique of Potiphar's wife.

39:20   Joseph was not executed, which was the usual punishment for his alleged crime. This may have been a reflection of the goodwill Joseph had earned by his previous service.

39:21-23   God was with Joseph in prison and Joseph was successful.

40:1-23   The dreams of the cupbearer and the baker.

40:1   The cupbearer and baker were high officials at Pharaoh's court.

40:3   The captain of the guard was responsible for the 2 prisoners. See 39:1 for the identity of the captain of the guard. Already God's hand can be seen controlling events.

40:8   Dreams were understood to be predictions of the future. Note how Joseph gives glory to God.

40:23   The cupbearer is restored to his original position and in all the rejoicing forgets Joseph's plea (40:14-15).

Lesson Aim:
To teach that God was with Joseph in every situation.

Lesson Plan

Start with pictures of children in different situations, e.g. playing in the park, at school, asleep, etc. As you show each picture ask the children if God knows what they are doing in that situation? Does God look after them when they are doing that thing? Is God everywhere? Revise the memory verse.

Remind the children of last week's story, using a question and answer format. Joseph was a long way from home. Would God be able to look after him in Egypt?

At the end of the story recap on the bad things that had happened to Joseph - put in the pit, sold as a slave to Potiphar, imprisoned. Was God with Joseph in all those situations? How do we know that is true?

Visual Aids

Pictures cut out of magazines of children in different situations, e.g. playing in the park, crossing the street, at school, asleep, etc.

Flannelgraph or pictures. You will need Potiphar, his wife, Joseph, the warder, the cupbearer and the baker.

Activities / 3 - 5s

Make a booklet. Photocopy pages 15 and 16 for each child. Prior to the lesson cut out the 2 dreams from page 15. Fold page 16 in half with the picture on the outside to give a 4 page booklet. Inside write along the top left hand side, *The wine steward had a dream.* Along the top right hand side write, *The chief baker had a dream.* Along the bottom write, *God told Joseph the meaning of the dreams.* The children glue the 2 dreams onto the inside of the booklet, then colour.

Activities / 5 - 7s

Photocopy page 17 on card for each child. Cut out all 3 circles. Cut along the solid line to the middle of the 2 large circles. On the back of the 2 large circles, starting at the slit, write the memory verse around the edge. Using a split pin paper fastener through the middle, attach the 3 circles together with the arrows on top and the small circle on the bottom.

Pull the middle circle through the slit in the top circle to show what happened to Joseph. The children colour the circles and draw a sad or happy mouth on each picture of Joseph.

Activities / 7 - 9s

Discuss the following situations with the children, bringing out the following points:
1. how they feel at the time.
2. how they are tempted to react.
3. how it helps to know that God is with them in the situation.
4. what God is teaching them through the situation.

Situation 1
Mary has been boasting about how good she is at .... (pick a sport/subject that applies to the class). One of Mary's friends fails at the same sport/subject. Mary says, "Oh, Jane, you are stupid!" Jan is very upset and tells the other children in the class what Mary said. The other children decide to gang up on Mary. They call her names and refuse to play with her. Mary is a Christian.

Situation 2
John sits next to Richard at school. The teacher gives the class some work to do and tells them not to talk to each other. Richard asks John a question and John answers. The teacher notices John talking and gives him a punishment (use an appropriate punishment, e.g. lines or a detention). John starts to make excuses but the teacher refuses to listen. Richard says nothing. John is a Christian.

Situation 3
Alison is having a birthday treat - she can take 4 friends to the cinema and then to McDonalds. She tells Tracy that she will be one of the four. Tracy is very excited. One week later, when the invitations are delivered, Tracy does not get one. Tracy is a Christian, but is still very disappointed.

14

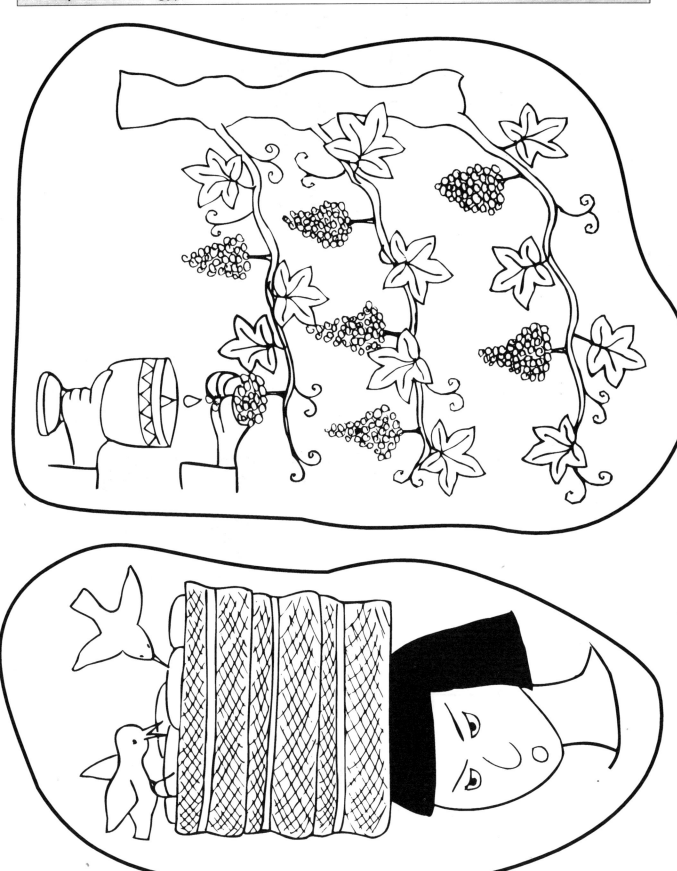

The Lord will hear
when I call to him.

Psalm 4:3

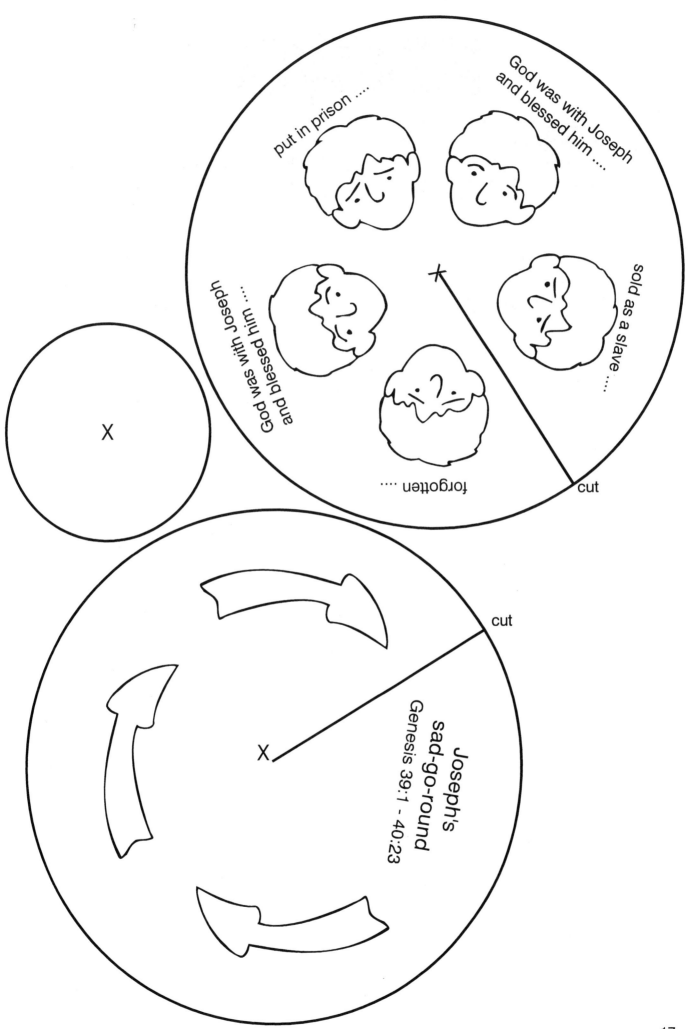

put in prison ....

God was with Joseph and blessed him ....

sold as a slave ....

God was with Joseph and blessed him ....

.... forgotten

cut

X

cut

X

Joseph's sad-go-round
Genesis 39:1 - 40:23

Preparation:
Read Genesis 41:1-57, using the Bible study notes to help you.

41:1	Note the time lapse.
41:14	The change of clothes and shaving were part of Egyptian court custom.
41:16	Joseph gave God the glory - see also Daniel 2:27-30.
41:29-31	The 7 years of famine are recorded in Egyptian historical records.
41:33-44	The court recognised the great wisdom of Joseph's answer. This, together with the interpretation of the dream, convinced them of Joseph's supernatural insight.
	Joseph's office was probably that of Grand Vizier. Other non-Egyptians were recorded as having gained similar positions in Egypt in the period 2,000 - 1,000 BC.
41:38	Note the change in Joseph from chapter 37 - not only is he wise and discerning, but also 'one in whom is the Spirit of God'.
41:42	The gold chain and robes of fine linen signified Joseph's important position. The signet ring allowed him to sign papers in the name of Pharaoh.
41:45	Joseph made a cultural adjustment - he changed his name to an Egyptian one and married an Egyptian wife. However, he still kept his faith in the God of Abraham (v.50-52).
41:46	Joseph was 17 years old when the story started. He is now 30. God had used those years in slavery and prison to refine Joseph and prepare him for his position of power in Egypt.

Lesson Aim:
To show how God gets Joseph into a position where he can save God's people from starvation.

41:53-57	It came to pass just as God had said. God put Joseph in the right place at the right time, and the Pharaoh listened and acted. The famine was severe and Joseph, as Governor of Egypt, operated a system of famine relief, selling grain to the people of Egypt (41:56) and subsequently to other countries (41:57). Joseph's preparations had been well laid.

Lesson Plan

Start with a simple quiz to see what the children have remembered from the previous 2 weeks. Split the children into 2 teams. Pin up on the board a palm tree trunk cut from brown paper for each team (see diagram).

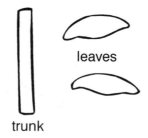

leaves

trunk

Each team also requires 5/6 palm leaves cut from green paper. In advance prepare 12-14 questions on the previous 2 lessons. The teams take it in turns to answer the questions. When a right answer is given a palm leaf is added to that team's palm tree. The first team to get all their palm leaves on their tree is the winner. If both teams achieve this on the same round, a draw is declared. Use the end of the quiz to lead into today's story.

At the end of the story point out the difference in Joseph's circumstances from when he lived in Canaan. In the normal course of events would Joseph have become Governor of Egypt? Go over the way God used circumstances to get Joseph where he wanted him. Revise the memory verse if not done as part of the quiz.

Visual Aids

Pictures or flannelgraph. You need Joseph, the cupbearer, Pharaoh, Pharaoh's dreams, some wise men (optional).

Activities / 3 - 5s

Photocopy pages 20 and 21 for each child. Prior to the lesson cut off the strip containing the fat cows from page 20 and cut along the thick black line around the thin cows' mouths on page 21.

The children colour both pictures. Concertina fold the fat cows strip lengthways and sellotape the right hand side together. (An adult will have to do this.) Fan out the left hand side of the strip so that the fat cows are visible. Thread the sellotaped end of the strip through the mouths of the thin cows. Pull the fat cows through the thin cows to see them swallowed up.

Activities / 5 - 7s

Follow instructions on page 22.

Activities / 7 - 9s

Photocopy page 24 for each child. Each child also requires an envelope containing a set of 9 counters. The counters are rectangles measuring 4 x 1.5 cm cut from paper. Write the following statements, one on each rectangle;

- *Pharaoh has a dream.*
- *Pharaoh is worried.*
- *Magicians and wise men.*
- *No meaning given.*
- *Wine steward remembers Joseph.*
- *A wise plan for the future.*
- *Joseph is sent for.*
- *Joseph gives God the glory.*
- *Joseph tells the meaning of the dream.*

The children glue the statements in the order of the story onto the steps to get Joseph from prison to being Prime Minister. Do this as a corporate activity, using it as a way of revising the story.

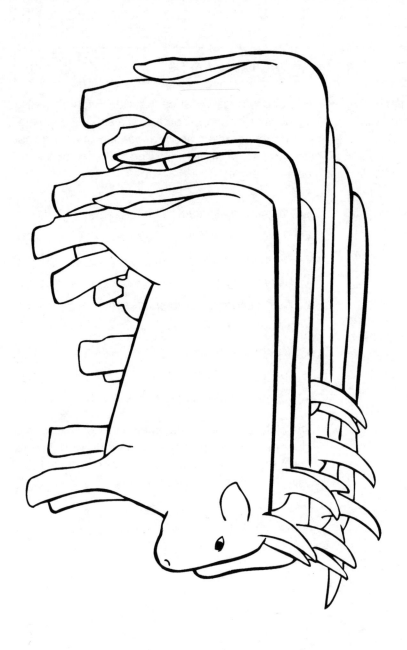

God showed Joseph the meaning of Pharaoh's dream.

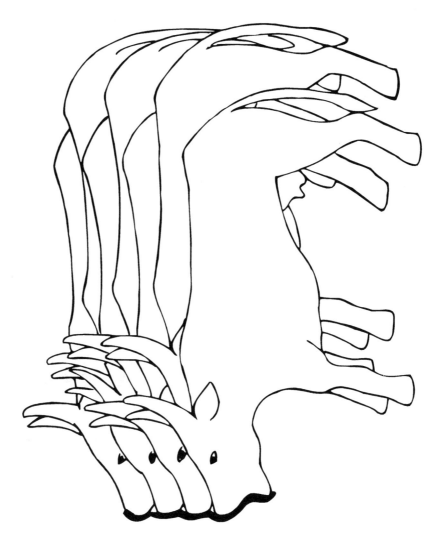

The Lord will hear when I call to him.   Psalm 4:3

Revision Game   This game is used to revise the details of the Bible story.
Photocopy pages 22 and 23 for each child and page 22 for the teacher.
Prior to the lesson cut out a set of 6 counters for each child and a complete set for the teacher. Give each child a different combination of counters and place them in an envelope.

1. Give each child page 23 and their envelope of counters.
2. Use the master set of counters to ensure that the children understand the meaning of each symbol.
3. Ask the questions in the order given. Any child with the correct answer holds up the counter.
   All correct answers are placed on the first vacant step on the game board.
4. The game continues until 1 child gets all 6 counters on the steps.
5. The counters can be mixed up and reallocated for a repeat of the game.

Questions

1. How many years did Joseph spend in prison after the wine steward was released?

2. What was Pharaoh's first dream?

3. What was Pharaoh's second dream?

4. For whom did Pharaoh send?

5. Could the wise men and magicians help Pharaoh?

6. Who remembered Joseph?

7. Who did Joseph say was the only one who could interpret dreams?

8. How many years of famine were to come?

9. Who gave Pharaoh a wise plan for the future?

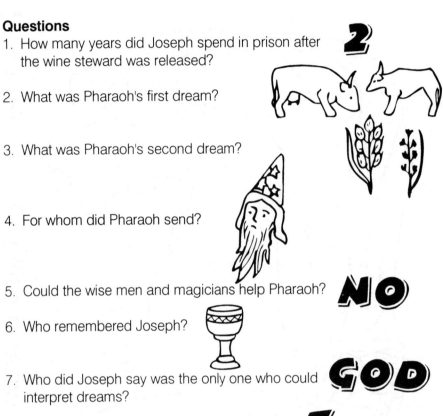

counters

Place your answers on the steps to get Joseph from prison to being Prime Minister

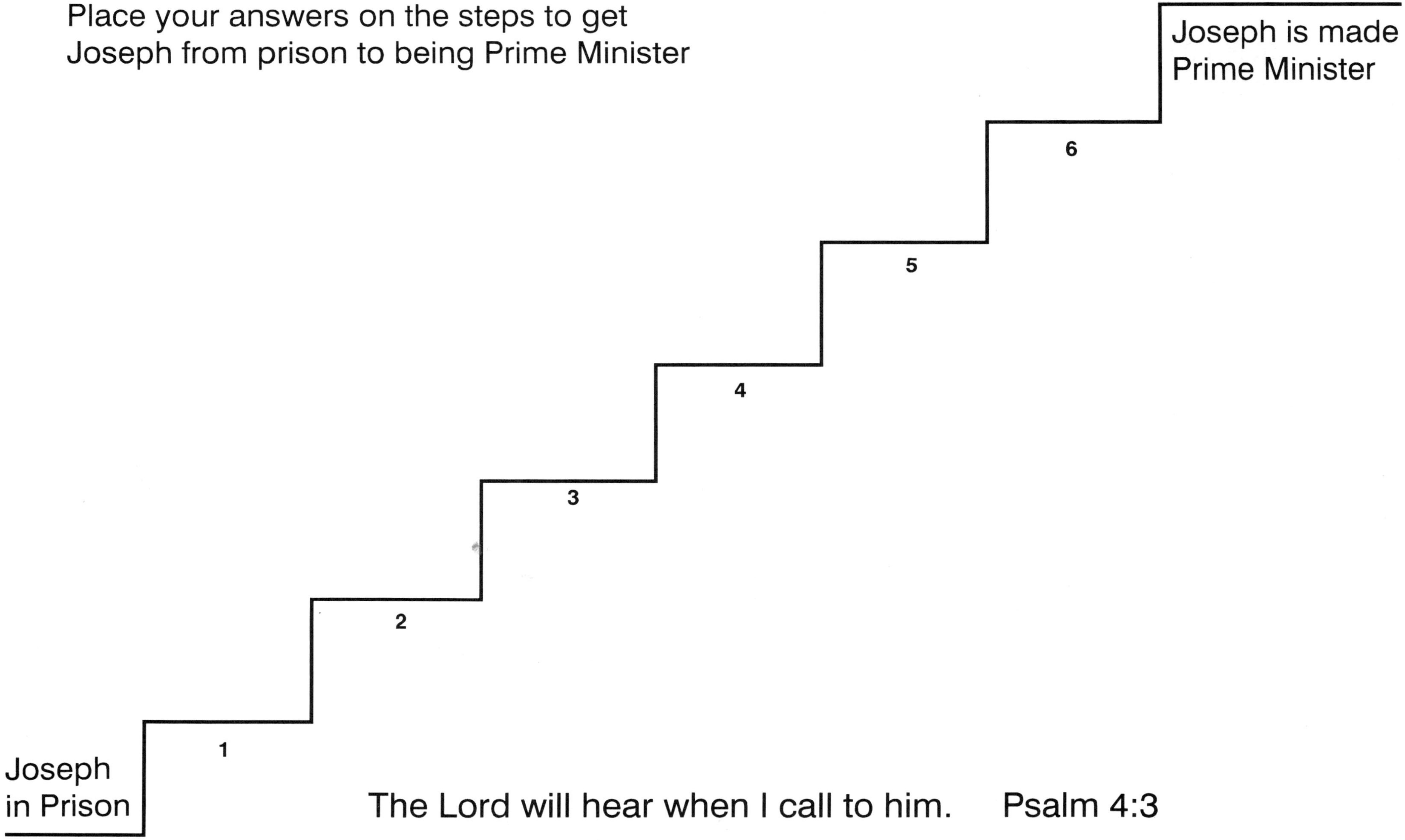

Joseph is made Prime Minister

6

5

4

3

2

1

Joseph in Prison

The Lord will hear when I call to him.   Psalm 4:3

23

Put the 9 counters in the right order up the steps to get Joseph from prison to being Prime Minister.

Joseph in Prison

Joseph is made Prime Minister

The Lord will hear when I call to him.   Psalm 4:3

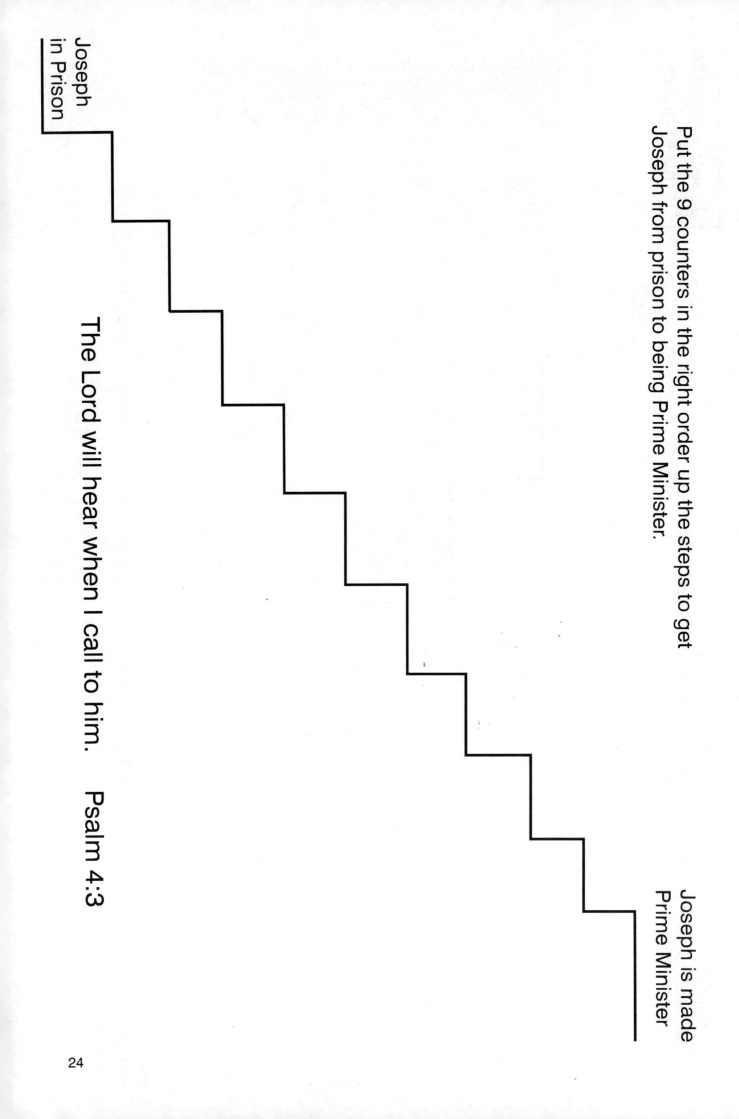

Preparation:
Read Genesis 42:1 - 46:7, using the Bible study notes to help you.

Lesson Aim:
To see the fulfillment of God's plan for Joseph.

42:4 — Benjamin has taken Joseph's place as his father's favourite.

42:7-17 — Joseph tested his brothers to see if they had changed. He was not seeking revenge.

42:21-22 — The brothers recognised God's hand in the situation and that they were being punished because of their treatment of Joseph all those years before.

42:24 — Joseph still loved his brothers (see also 42:25-26).

42:36 — Jacob dissolved into self-pity.

42:37 — Note the change in Reuben from chapter 37. He is now prepared to take responsibility for his youngest brother.

43:6 — Note Jacob is here called Israel - his covenant name. He was still blaming the 10 brothers for what had happened.

43:8-9 — Note the change in Judah from 37:26-27.

43:11-14 — God used circumstances to bring Jacob to the point of capitulation - he must trust God for the future of his sons.

44:1-5 — The steward is in Joseph's confidence.

44:13 — The brothers returned to Joseph's house. This time there is no thought of deserting their father's favourite (see 44:10).

44:16 — Judah recognised God's hand in the situation.

44:18-29 — Judah related the history of their dealings with Joseph.

44:30-33 — Note the change in Judah. He was prepared to take personal charge of

Benjamin, his father's favourite, and was keen to protect his father from further misery. He was willing to offer himself in place of Benjamin (see 43:9).

45:3 — The brothers must have thought their last hour had come. (See 50:15-21 for what happened when Jacob died.)

45:5 — Joseph was conscious of God's hand in everything that had happened, but this did not mean that the brothers were not responsible for their actions (42:21-22).

45:22 — Note that Benjamin was still being favoured.

45:24 — Joseph gave his brothers a practical admonition!

46:1 — Beersheba was the place where God appeared to Hagar (21:14-19) and where Abraham called on the name of God, the Eternal One (21:33).

46:3-4 — Note God's promise to Jacob.

Lesson Plan

Start by reminding the children of the previous 3 lessons on Joseph. Revise the memory verse. Look at how Joseph has changed since he left home. Point out to the children how much time has passed. Perhaps Joseph's father and brothers have changed as well.

At the end of the story point out to the older children how Joseph foreshadows Jesus. He was hated and sold by his brothers, but ended up saving them from dying of starvation. The brothers recognised their guilt, were unable to save themselves, and had to accept the offered salvation.

Visual Aids

- pictures of the main characters.
- 11 sacks of grain (plastic bags filled with old newspaper - the bags must be big enough to contain the cup and must be opaque). Each sack is labelled with one of the brothers' names.
- 11 pieces of material tied at the neck to form money bags.
- 1 goblet.

The sacks are produced at the appropriate moment in the story and looked in one at a time to find the goblet. (Sacks need to be prepared before the lesson.) The younger children will not know whose sack is supposed to contain the goblet).

Activities / 3 - 5s

Follow the instructions on page 28.

Activities / 5 - 7s

Photocopy pages 29-39 for each child. Staple pages 29-38 together on the right hand side to form a book. Cut off the marked areas on sheets 30-37. Cut out the pictures from sheet 39 and place in an envelope for each child.

The children glue the pictures onto the appropriate pages in the book. This is best done as a corporate activity. At the end, go through the book pointing out that, whereas Joseph could only see the story as it unfolded, God had planned it all before it happened. It was only with hindsight that Joseph could see how God had controlled events (Genesis 50:20).

Activities / 7 - 9s

Make a Joseph Pyramid. Photocopy page 40 on card for each child. Complete the pyramid as a corporate activity, using it to revise details of Joseph's life.

1. Cut out the shape from page, score and fold along the dotted lines.
2. Colour the 'years' triangle using a different colour for each section.
3. Start at the bottom of the 'Joseph' triangle:
(a) Where did Joseph live as a boy? Colour the bottom section the same as the bottom section of the 'years' triangle and write 'Canaan'.
(b) How old was Joseph when he was sold as a slave? The children check their answer by looking at the 'years' triangle. Check by reading Genesis 37:2.
(c) How long was Joseph a slave and in prison? (Genesis 41:46) Colour the next section the same as the corresponding section on the 'years' triangle and write 'slave and prisoner'.
(d) What position did Joseph hold when he came out of prison? Colour the top section and write 'Governor of all Egypt'.
4. Look at the 'years' triangle. What happened during the first 14 years when Joseph was governor? Write 'famine' and 'plenty' in the correct places.
5. Start at the bottom of 'Jacob's family' triangle:
(a) Where did Jacob's family live? Colour the bottom section the same colour as the bottom section of 'Joseph' triangle and write 'Canaan'.
(b) How many years of famine were left when Jacob and family went to Egypt to live? The children give the answer by looking at the pyramid. Read Genesis 45:6 to check the answer is correct.
(c) How old was Jacob when he went to Egypt? (Genesis 47:9) Fill in the age on the triangle.
(d) Who died aged 147 years? (Genesis 47:28) Fill in the name on the triangle.
6. Look at the 'Joseph' triangle. How old was Joseph when he died? (Genesis 50:22) Fill in the answer on the triangle.
7. Fold the pyramid along the dotted lines and glue together with the flap on the inside.

In which sack is the cup?

The Lord will hear when I call to him.

Psalm 4:3

Photocopy pages 27 and 28 for each child.
Prior to the lesson, cut along the solid lines round the outside of the sacks on page 27 and bend back along dotted lines. Write the 11 brother's names on sticky labels, 1 set for each child, for the children to stick onto the sacks.

The children colour the cup on page 28, then glue this page behind page 27, only gluing at the edges so that the sacks can be opened to see what is in them. Stick the names onto each sack, making sure Benjamin's name is on the sack containing the goblet. Go through the sacks, asking the children, 'Is the cup in ....'s sack?' The children open up the sack to find out. The insides of the sacks can be coloured yellow to represent corn.

The Story of Joseph

cut off

Joseph is Jacob's favourite son.
His brothers hate him.

cut off

Joseph's brothers sell him to some traders. He becomes a slave in Egypt.

cut off

Potiphar's wife tells lies about Joseph. He is put in prison.

cut off

Pharaoh's wine steward and baker are put in prison also. They both have a dream. Joseph tells them what the dreams mean.

cut off

2 years later Pharaoh has
a dream. No-one can tell him
what it means.

cut off

The wine steward tells Pharaoh about Joseph. Joseph tells Pharaoh what his dream means.

cut off

Joseph tells Pharaoh how to prevent the coming famine from destroying Egypt. Joseph is made Prime Minister.

cut off

The famine affects Canaan as well as Egypt. Jacob's family are starving. They come to Egypt for food.

1.

2.

3.

4.

5.

6.

7.

8.

Joseph tells his brothers:
'God sent me ahead of you
to rescue you ....'
Genesis 45:7

38

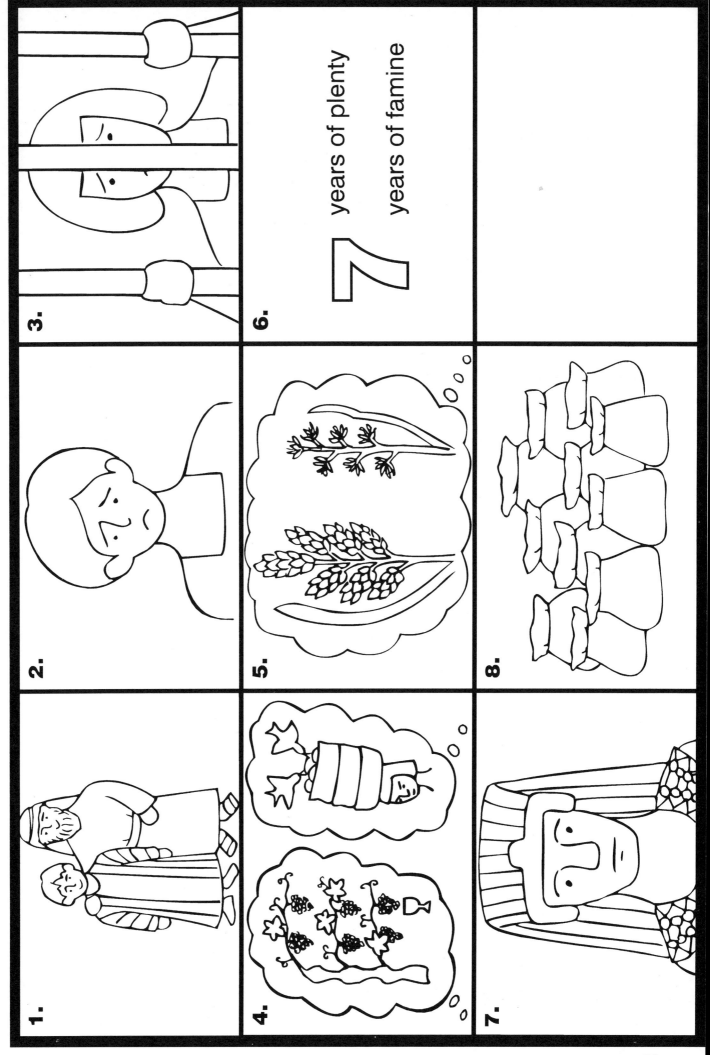

3.

6.

7
years of plenty
years of famine

2.

5.

8.

1.

4.

7.

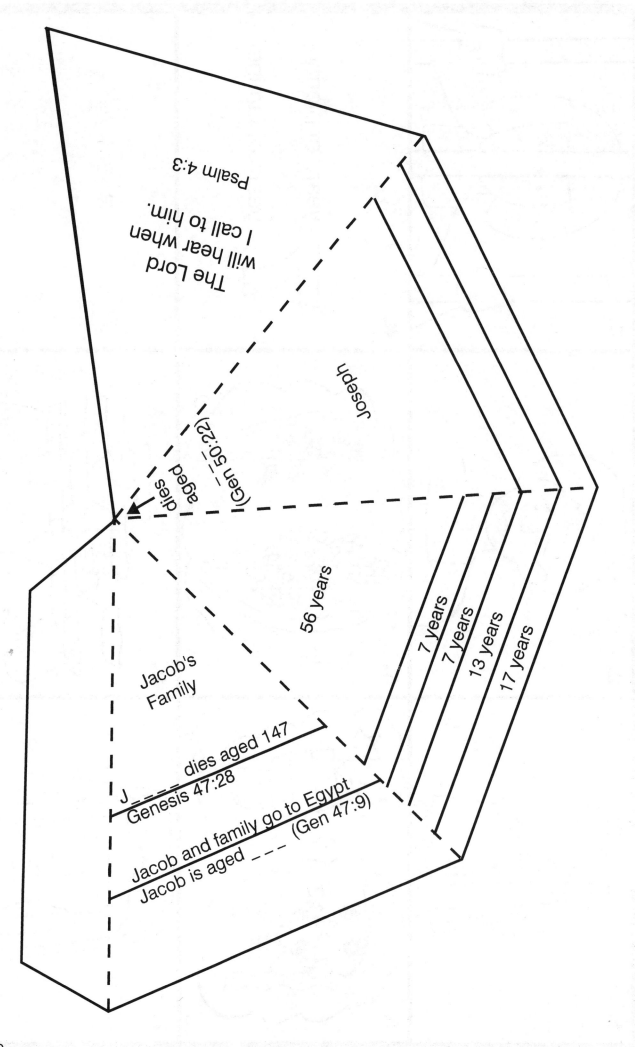

Psalm 4:3

The Lord
will hear when
I call to him.

Joseph

dies aged
(Gen 50:22)

56 years

7 years
7 years
13 years
17 years

Jacob's
Family

dies aged 147
J_ _ _ _ _
Genesis 47:28

Jacob and family go to Egypt
Jacob is aged _ _ _ (Gen 47:9)

Job

Overview

JOB
Job 1:1 - 2:10; 42:10-17

To learn that God is in control, so we can trust him to care for us in difficult situations.

Series Aims

1. To understand that God is in control of every aspect of our lives.

2. To learn that we can trust God to care for us in difficult situations.

The story of Job is about a good man who loses possessions, children and health. His wife and friends interpret this as God's judgment on his sin and Job becomes an outcast. His friends explain his suffering in traditional religious terms (in Job's day material prosperity was a sign of God's blessing), but fail to offer Job any comfort or hope. Eventually God appears to Job - but not to answer his questions. Instead, God portrays his great power and might (Job 38:1 - 41:34) and shows Job that his concept of God was too small. Job's reaction is to repent and worship (Job 42:1-6). The book ends with Job's prosperity restored by God.

The story is about a real man (Ezekiel 14:14, James 5:11), who is thought to be contemporary with Isaac and Jacob - his wealth was tied up in livestock rather than money. He was a priest to his own family (Job 1:5), which is another indicator that he lived before Moses and the establishment of the Levitical priesthood.

The book deals with the problem of suffering and God's sovereignty. If God is just and good why does he allow the innocent to suffer? The only answer we are given is that God is all powerful and there is nothing outside his control. Job did not understand why he suffered - but God enabled him to come through the time of trial.

Very young children have no problems with this story - God is God and can do what he likes. It is the 7-9 year olds who raise the question of, 'why?'

Memory work

3-5s   In all things God works for good.
       Romans 8:28

5-9s   In all things God works for the good of those who love him.
       Romans 8:28

Lesson Aim:
To understand that God is in control of every
aspect of our lives and we can trust him to care
for us in difficult situations.

*Note. He is given twice as many animals and the
same number of children as he previously had. This
does not teach that God's people will always be
blessed on earth - our inheritance is in heaven
(Hebrews 11:13-16, 2 Corinthians 5:1).*

1:1	Uz - the exact location is unknown.
1:4	These may have been birthday feasts.
1:5	Job was aware that purity came from the heart.
1:12	Satan's power is controlled by God - he was only allowed to attack Job's possessions, not his person.
1:15	Sabeans - a group of nomadic raiders who eventually settled in Sheba..
1:17	Chaldeans - nomads from south Mesopotamia (Abraham's homeland).
1:21	Job demonstrates his complete trust in God.
2:4-5	Satan says Job is only really concerned for himself.
2:6	Again we see God is in ultimate control.
2:11 - 42:9	This needs to be summarised briefly for the children so that the story makes sense. E.g. Job's three friends told him that he must have done something wrong for God to send such suffering, but Job would not listen; he knew he had done nothing wrong. Job called on God to answer him, and eventually God did so. God appeared to Job in all his power and majesty and Job was sorry for what he had said. 'I know, Lord, that you are all-powerful;' Job said. 'You can do everything you want.'
42:10-17	God vindicates Job by blessing him.

Lesson Plan

Start by asking the children if
they can remember the name of Joseph's father.
What animals did he have? Today's true story from
the Bible is about a man who lived around the same
time as Jacob. He was a very rich man and had lots of
animals. The younger children can be asked to make
the noise of the sheep, cows and donkeys.

At the end of the story teach the memory verse. How
do we know that God was in control of what happened
to Job? - the Bible tells us so. It is the 7-9s who have
most difficulty with this story, because it does not
seem fair. Some of them may be having difficulties at
school because of their Christian faith and these
often find the story of Job a help.

Visual Aids

Start with a picture of Job. To illustrate his animals
and children have pictures of seven sons, 3
daughters (you can use cut-out chain people stuck
onto card), 1 sheep, 1 cow, 1 donkey and 1 camel.
(See the activity for 3-5s on page 44. Enlarge the
pictures, glue onto card and colour.) Pin them up to
the left of Job as you talk, (for young children just say
'lots of sheep', etc; for older ones you can give the
numbers). Describe the scene in heaven - you do not
need pictures, but use your voice to make it exciting
and awesome.

As the various messengers come to Job, remove the

...ate pictures from the board. Have a picture ...ob sitting dejectedly, covered with boils for the ...in disease. At the end, replace the Job with boils with the original picture of Job. As God restores his possessions, have pictures of 7 sons, 3 daughters, 2 sheep, 2 cows, 2 camels and 2 donkeys ready to pin up. This brings home to the children that God has doubled his animals.

Activities / 3 - 5s

Each child requires a photocopy of page 44 and an A4 sheet of coloured paper. Fold the sheet of coloured paper in 3 and cut out the hatched area (see diagram). Write the memory verse along the bottom as shown. Fold in C and write Job trusted God. Fold A over C and write Job on the outside. Cut out Job and the animals from the photocopied page and place in an envelope for each child. Cut out the 2 strips and make the chain boys and girls.

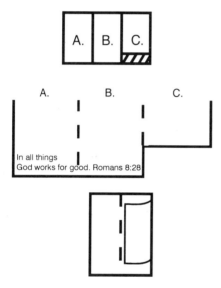

The children glue Job above the Bible verse on A and the animals, sons and daughters on B and C. The 7 sons will need to go across B and C. The people and animals can be coloured if time permits.

Activities / 5 - 7s

Cut a circle of coloured card for each child approximately 10 cm in diameter. Write 'In God I trust.' in the centre. Attach a safety pin to the back of the card circle to make a badge. The children decorate their badges.

Activities / 7 - 9s

Each child requires a paper plate, 1 yoghurt pot or disposable cup to be the body, 1 egg carton section for a head, wool for hair, and 4 strips of paper long enough to make sleeves to go over the yoghurt pot or disposable cup.

Prior to the lesson write on the centre of the plate (the right way up), *God cared for Job in his troubles. He lost his animals, but he still trusted in God. Then he lost his children, but he still trusted in God. Then he was covered with sores, but he still trusted in God. God was pleased that Job trusted in him even when things went wrong. God gave Job back all that he had lost and lots more.*

The children sellotape the egg carton section onto the top of the pot/cup. Draw a face on the egg carton section and glue on wool for hair. Turn the paper plate over and sellotape the bottom of the pot/cup to the centre of the underside of the plate. Write the memory verse round the rim. On each of the 4 strips of paper write the word and draw pictures from the following list - one category per strip.

- family - discuss times when the child is at odds with other family members.

- friends - discuss breaking up with friends.

- house - discuss times when the child is away from home.

- sick - discuss when the child is sick.

Join the edges of the strips together with sellotape to make sleeves to fit the body attached to the plate. Place all 4 sleeves on the body. Explain to the children that they can use them as a reminder to pray. If someone is sick put the sick sleeve on top, if praying for friends put the friends sleeve on top, etc.

A.

B.

Fold strip A along dotted line, then concertina fold and cut around the figure to make a chain of seven boys.

Fold strip B along dotted line, then concertina fold and cut around figure to make a chain of three girls.

Moses

Week 6	GOD PROVIDES A DELIVERER To teach that God is in control.	*Exodus 1:1 - 2:10*
Week 7	GOD PREPARES A DELIVERER To show how God equips his servant for the job God gives him to do.	*Exodus 3:1 - 4:17*
Week 8	GOD DEMONSTRATES HIS POWER To teach that God's plan cannot be thwarted.	*Exodus 5:1 - 10:29*
Week 9	GOD DELIVERS HIS PEOPLE To show how God saves his people from death and slavery in Egypt.	*Exodus 11:1 - 12:42*
Week 10	GOD DESTROYS HIS ENEMIES To show how God saves his people from destruction.	*Exodus 13:17 - 14:31*

Series Aims

1. To understand the stories in their context.

2. To understand that God is in control of every aspect of our lives - bad as well as good.

Moses was raised up by God to deliver his people from Egypt, bind them into a nation, and lead them to the Promised Land. He was equipped as a leader through early training in the Egyptian court (Acts 7:22), and, more importantly, through being a close follower of God by faith (Hebrews 11:23-29, Acts 7:23-37). He was both prophet and law-giver, being the model of all later prophets, and was called by God to make known God's will to God's people (Exodus 3:1-4:17). Moses, as representative of the Old Testament law, stood with Jesus on the Mount of Transfiguration.

The Israelites had been living in Egypt for nearly 400 years. During that time God had blessed them with a great increase in numbers (Exodus 1:7). Goshen was a fertile land and a good place in which to live (Genesis 47:5-6). But God's purpose was to have a people for himself, and he had promised them Canaan for their inheritance (Genesis 17:7-8), so he used the sufferings inflicted on them by the new king of Egypt to make them want to leave. This king unknowingly carried out God's will, and his 3 attempts to reduce the growth of Israel all failed (Exodus 1:12; 1:15-17; 1:22-2:10).

The story of Moses is an example of God's sovereignty.

Memory work

3-5s	In all things God works for good. *Romans 8:28*	**5-9s**	In all things God works for the good of those who love him. *Romans 8:28*

45

WEEK 6
God Provides a Deliverer

Preparation:
Read Exodus 1:1 - 2:10, using the Bible study notes to help you.

Lesson Aim:
To teach that God is in control.

1:7 This was amazing growth - the 70 who had come to Egypt had become at least 600,000 in 400 years (Exodus 12:37).

1:13 An unreasonable amount of work was expected, and failure to reach the targets resulted in punishment.

1:15 These were the 2 principal midwives - there would probably have been more than 2 for so large a community.

1:16 The boys would grow up to be soldiers, so must be killed. The girls would be absorbed into Egyptian families through marriage. Eventually the Hebrew race would die out.

1:19 Were the midwives lying? Or were they just making sure they arrived too late? You need to have given this some thought, because some children may ask, 'Is it all right to lie?'

2:1 For the names of Moses' family see Numbers 26:59.

2:2 The beauty of the baby was taken by the parents as a sign from God that something special was intended for him (Hebrews 11:23).

2:6 God used the baby's tears and beauty to move the princess to show compassion on him.

2:10 God ensured that Moses, in his early years, was instructed in the true faith by his parents, before being adopted into the king's household, where he lived for 40 years (Acts 7:22-23).

Lesson Plan

This is the first lesson of a new series. Start by showing the children pictures of pyramids, palm trees, the sun in a blue sky. Ask them if the country in the pictures is a hot or a cold country. The older children can be asked if they can identify the country. Tell the children the country is called Egypt. Ask them if they can remember from 2 weeks ago who lived in Egypt. Point out that 400 years had passed since Joseph was alive. The king of Egypt did not know about Joseph. Tell the story.
At the end of the story point out how God saved Moses from being killed. Teach the memory verse.

Visual Aids

Tell the story from Moses' mother's viewpoint. You will need a baby doll, a basket (this can be a shoe box

appropriately coloured), a strip of blue paper or cloth to be the river.
Alternatively, use pictures or flannelgraph.
Children like acting out this story.

Activities / 3 - 5s

The children will make a model of Moses in the basket. Each child requires 1 toilet roll or 1/2 paper towel cardboard tube, 1 wooden clothes peg, 1 paper tissue, 1 rubber band, scraps of material and shapes x, y and z cut from dark brown or black adhesive plastic (available from Woolworth's and DIY shops). Prior to the lesson cut out one each of shapes x and y and two of shape z for each child (see templates on page 48). Also cut the top third off the cardboard tube (see diagram).

- Using the 2 z shapes seal both ends of the cardboard tube (see diagram).
- Cover the tube with shape x (see diagram).
- Wrap the clothes peg in the tissue and secure with a rubber band (see diagram). Draw a face on the clothes peg (this will need to be done by an adult).
- Line the tube with scraps of material for bedding and place the baby inside. Cover tube with shape y (see diagram).

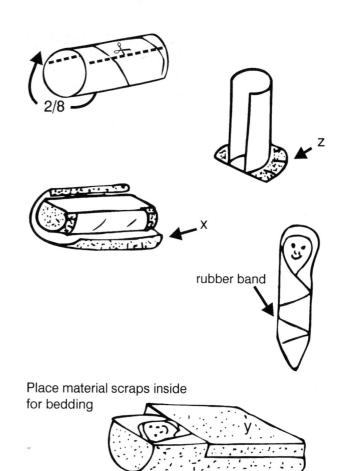

rubber band

Place material scraps inside for bedding

Activities / 5 - 7s

Make a picture dome. Photocopy pages 49 and 50 for each child. Prior to the lesson cut out all the pieces.

Instructions
- Colour the picture, the basket and the reeds.
- Fold the picture and side pieces along the dotted lines. Glue side piece A to the right hand side of the picture, starting at the base and bending it to fit. Glue side piece B to the left hand side of the picture, starting at the base. Glue B to A at the apex (see diagram).
- Fold the bottom sections on the reeds backwards along the dotted lines and glue in place on the base of the dome.
- Fold the basket tab backwards and the basket lid forwards to cover the baby. Glue the basket in place on the base of the dome (see diagram). The basket lid can fold down to cover the baby.
- If necessary, place a blob of bluetak on the base of the dome behind the basket to stabilise the dome.

Activities / 7 - 9s

Photocopy pages 51/52 back to back for each child. Do this as a class activity to prevent the less able from being left behind.

Templates

Prior to lesson:
Cut out shapes x,y and z, in
sticky-backed plastic for each
child.

cut slits

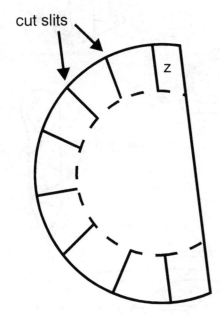

z

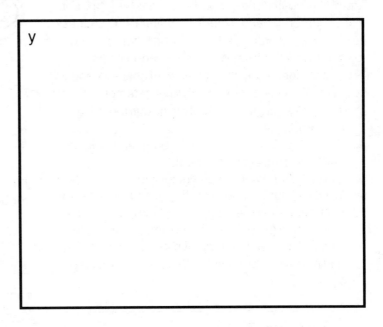

y

x

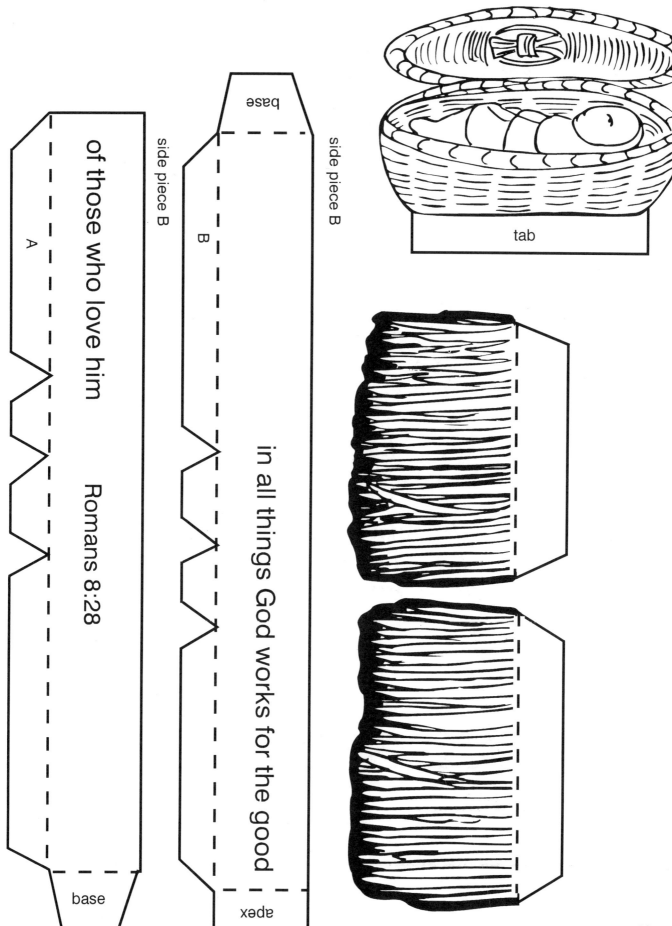

side piece B

A

of those who love him　　Romans 8:28

base

side piece B

B

base

side piece B

in all things God works for the good

apex

tab

reeds

reeds

basket

God's people were in trouble! Over 300 years had passed since Joseph came to Egypt. There were now so many Israelites that the Egyptians were frightened of them. So the Egyptians made them s.............. and treated them very cruelly.

But the Israelites continued to have more and more babies!

The King of Egypt made a plan ....

The 2 Israelite midwives were told -

"If the baby is a .... kill it!"

"If the baby is a .... let it live!"

Why did the King order only the boys to be killed?

Did the midwives obey the King? ☐ yes ☐ no

The Bible says, "For the sake of the Lord, submit to every human authority."

1 Peter 2:13

Were the midwives right?

The King gave a new order -

"Throw all the new-born Israelite boys into the river!"

To whom did the King give the order?

☐ the soldiers

☐ the midwives

☐ all the people

☐ the parents

Then ....

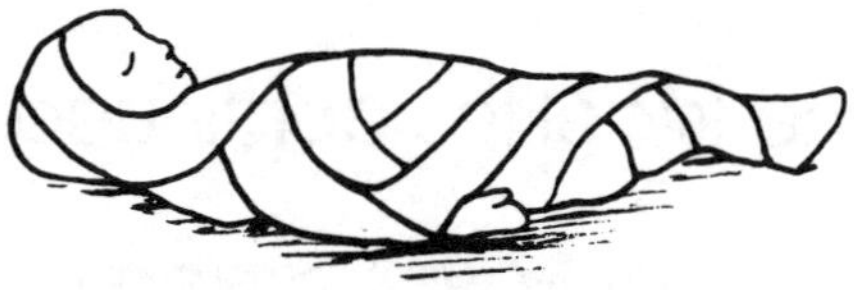

a baby boy was born.

The baby was beautiful. His mother hid him for .... months, until she could hide him no longer.

Then she did a very clever thing!

She took a .... made of .... and covered it with .... to make it watertight. She put the baby in the basket and left it in the tall .... at the edge of the ....

The King's daughter found the baby. She asked his mother to look after him until he was old enough to live in the King's palace. The princess called the baby,

'Moses'.

THINK SPOT

Did God know what was happening to his people?

How would the birth of a baby help?

Memory verse

In all things God works for the good of those who love him.

Romans 8:28

WEEK 7
God Prepares a Deliverer

Lesson Aim:
To show how God equips his servant for the job God gives him to do.

This incident took place when Moses was 80 years old, after 40 years of formal education in the royal court of Egypt and 40 years in the Arabian desert. 40 years previously Moses had tried to help his fellow Hebrews and failed and, as a result, had to flee from Pharaoh's anger (Exodus 2:11-16). He settled in Midian, working as a shepherd, and married one of Jethro's daughters. They had a son named Gershom (foreigner). During this time God was preparing Moses for the job he had in store for him. At the same time God caused the Hebrews to turn to him (God) for help (Exodus 2:23-25).

Note the objections Moses raised when told by God what he was to do -

1. his own unworthiness (Exodus 3:11)

2. his inability to tell the people who God is (Exodus 3:13)

3. the people would not believe him (Exodus 4:1)

4. his speech difficulty (Exodus 4:10)

5. he did not want to go (Exodus 4:13)

Also note how God refutes each objection.

3:2	No personal form of God appeared, but the flames and voice were sufficient evidence of God's presence.
3:5	In the East shoes are still removed before entering a holy place as a sign of reverence and personal unworthiness.
3:12	The proof was to be a future event.
3:13	'Name' here means credentials, nature, character.
3:14	The Hebrew word used in this title of God

implies all 3 tenses in English - past, present and future (Hebrew only has complete and incomplete actions). Bound up in this are the truths of God's self-existence, self-sufficiency, eternity and unchangeableness.

3:15	God also instructed Moses to use a name familiar to the Hebrews - the God of Abraham, Isaac and Jacob. They would have been familiar with the stories of God's dealings with these 3 and understood what they implied about God's character, e.g. he kept his word.
3:18	3 days' journey was necessary to avoid giving offence, as some of the sacrificial animals were sacred to the Egyptians
4:1	A natural objection - 400 years had passed since God had last revealed himself to his people (Genesis 46:2-4).
4:3	In Egypt the serpent was a symbol of royal power.
4:4	Grasping the snake by the tail was an act of faith; the normal way to pick up a snake is at the back of the neck to prevent it biting the handler.
4:10,13	Note the contradiction, 'No, Lord'.

Lesson Plan

See how much the children can remember from last week's story. Talk about what it means to be a slave. Ask the children what jobs slaves would do. Show pictures of the various things a slave might do, e.g. building work, carrying bricks, sweeping the floor and other household tasks. Instead of pictures you might like to ask the children to mime the various tasks. Use this to lead into the story.

At the end of the story go over the 5 objections Moses made and God's answers. For the older children, try and apply it to their own Christian service, e.g. telling a friend about Jesus. Finish by revising the memory verse.

Visual Aids

Flannelgraph or pictures. You need Moses, sheep, a bush with flames, and a staff and a serpent to interchange. There is very little action in this story so you need to use change of voice, tempo, etc. to keep it interesting for the children.

Activities / 3 - 5s

Make a story pyramid. Each child requires page 56 photocopied on paper and a card pyramid. To make the pyramid follow the instructions on page 55. The children colour the pictures and glue them around the pyramid in the order of the story.

Activities / 5 - 7s

Make a model of Moses at the burning bush. Follow the instructions on page 57.

Activities / 7 - 9s

Each child requires pages 58 and 59 photocopied on card and 2 split pin paper fasteners.

Instructions

- Cut out the shapes from page 59. Colour Moses and the burning bush if time permits.
- Fold Moses and the burning bush along the dotted lines with the tabs facing backwards.

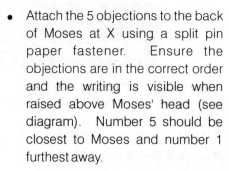

- Attach the 5 objections to the back of Moses at X using a split pin paper fastener. Ensure the objections are in the correct order and the writing is visible when raised above Moses' head (see diagram). Number 5 should be closest to Moses and number 1 furthest away.
- If Moses will not stay upright make a brace from a strip of card and staple it to the base and halfway between waist and feet (see diagram).
- Using a split pin paper fastener attach the wheel behind the bush so that the answers are visible in the gap as the wheel is turned.
- Glue Moses and the bush onto page 58 where indicated.
- Moses' objections can be raised one at a time and the correct response dialled up on the bush. The responses are not in the correct order so the children will need to use their Bibles to work out which answer is the right one.
- Fill in the memory verse and answer the questions on page 58.

Instructions
1. Use the template from this sheet to draw out the following shape onto light card.
2. Fold along dotted lines.
3. Glue flap a. to pyramid side.
4. Glue other flaps to pyramid base.
5. Colour pictures, cut out and glue in order around pyramid.

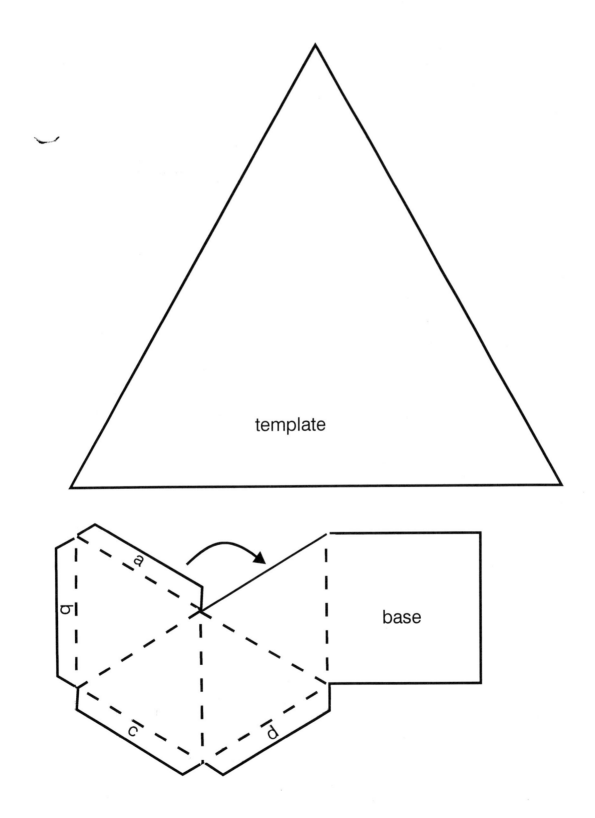

template

base

a

b

c

d

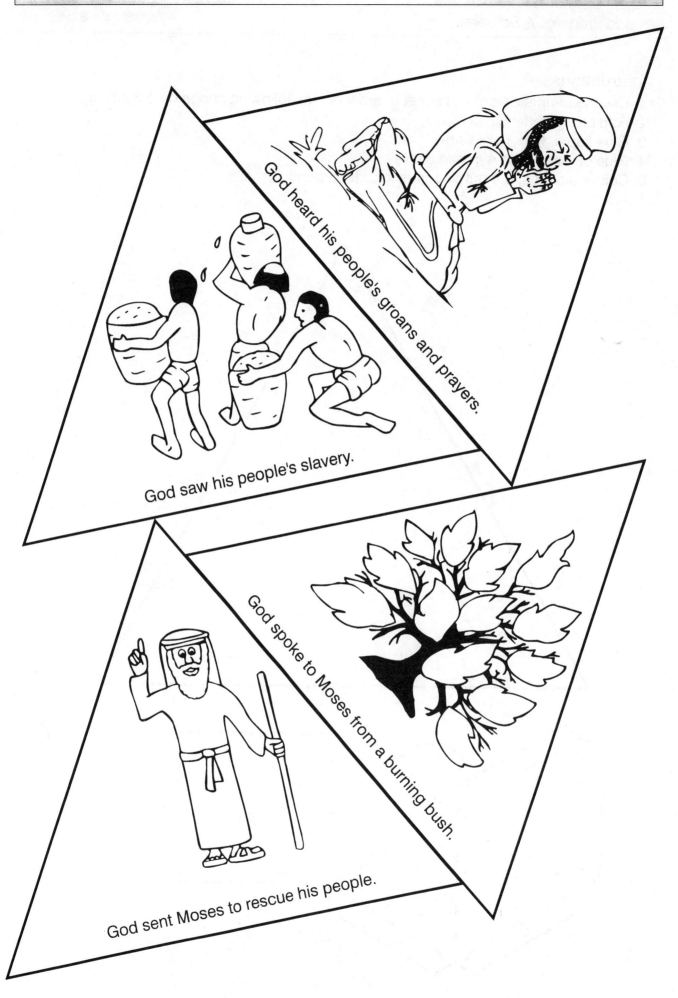

God heard his people's groans and prayers.

God saw his people's slavery.

God spoke to Moses from a burning bush.

God sent Moses to rescue his people.

Instructions

Requirements for each child
1. Block of oasis 8x10x3cm (obtainable from any florist)
2. 3 pipe cleaners
3. Pink gummed paper
4. Red tissue paper
5. Garden twigs
6. Material for robe
7. Rubber bands

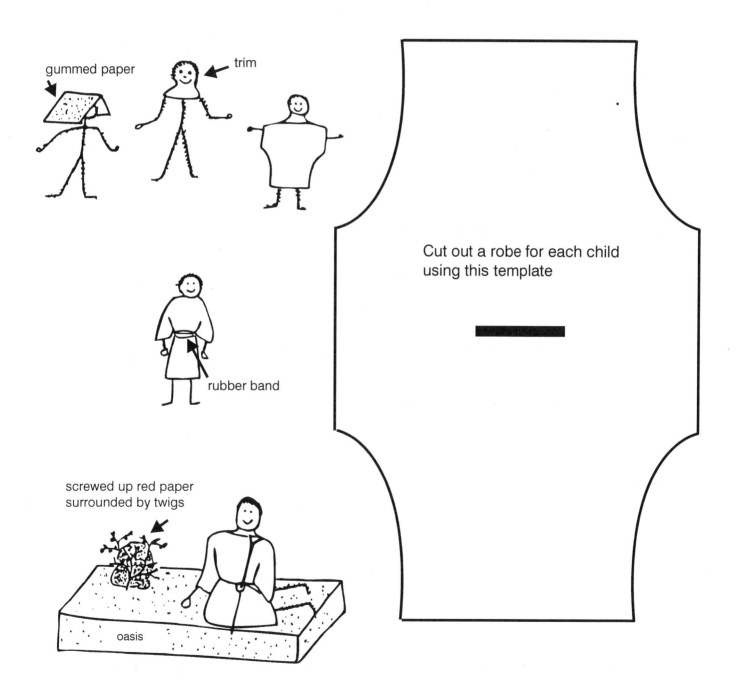

gummed paper

trim

rubber band

screwed up red paper surrounded by twigs

oasis

Cut out a robe for each child using this template

MOSES

bush
_____

God prepares a deliverer.

Exodus 3:1 - 4:17

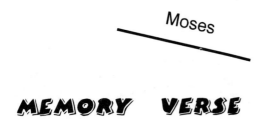

_____ Moses

MEMORY VERSE

How was this true of Moses' life to this point in time?

1. Exodus 1:22 - 2:10

2. Acts 7:22

3. Exodus 2:15-21

Look at the excuses Moses made and the way God answered him.

What can I learn from this?

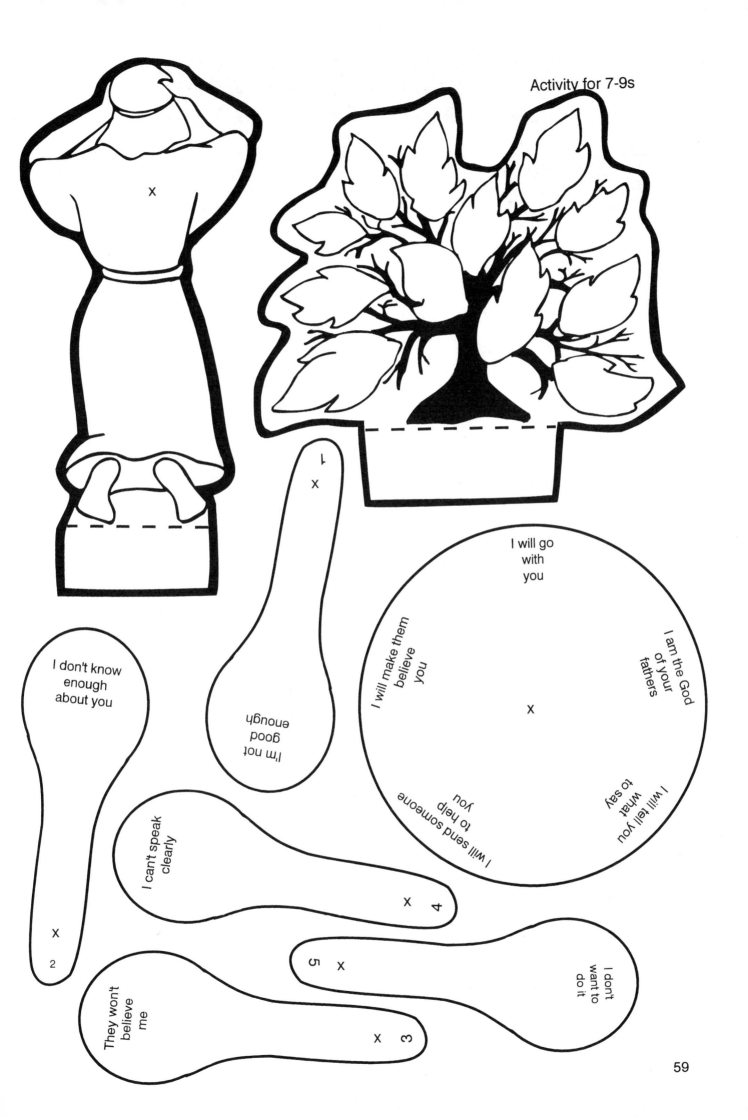

Activity for 7-9s

I will go
with
you

I am the God
of your
fathers

I will make them
believe
you

I will tell you
what
to say

I will send someone
to help
you

x

I don't know
enough
about you

I'm not
good
enough

x 1

I can't speak
clearly

They won't
believe
me

I don't
want to
do it

x 2

x 4

x 5

x 3

59

Preparation:
Read Exodus 5:1 - 10:29, using the
Bible study notes to help you.

Lesson Aim:
To teach that God's plan cannot
be thwarted.

This whole section deals with the way God answers Pharaoh's question in Exodus 5:2, 'Who is the Lord? Why should I listen to him?'

The plagues were announced beforehand so that believing Egyptians could act accordingly. God's justice is always tempered with mercy.

8:9	Pharaoh was asked to set the time when Moses was to pray so that there would be no question of coincidence.
8:18-19	The magicians recognised God's hand at work, but Pharaoh would not.
8:22	A distinction is made between the Egyptians and the Israelites.
8:25	Pharaoh tries to compromise.
9:18-19	The Egyptians were given the opportunity to escape the consequences of the plague if they believed God's word.

9:27	Pharaoh confessed his sin - but it did not result in a change of behaviour.
9:31-32	Note God's graciousness.
10:1-2	The reason for the miracles is that 'all of you will know that I am the Lord'. (The older children can be referred back to the series on Jesus demonstrating his authority in Book 2 - the miracles were to demonstrate who he was).
10:7-11	Pharaoh and the Egyptians still try to compromise (see also Exodus 10:24).

Lesson Plan

♦ Start by asking the children whom they listen to. Which people do they obey? Why? Talk about the actions taken by people in authority to demonstrate that they are in charge, e.g. punishment. Talk about God being in charge of everything and everyone.

What sort of things might God do to show that he is the boss? In today's true story from the Bible we will find out how God showed the king of Egypt who was boss. Tell the children to listen carefully so that they can tell you about 1 plague (or more, depending on ability of the group) at the end of the story.

At the end of the story go over the plagues and revise the memory verse. Discuss with the older children how God worked for good through the plagues, e.g. making a distinction between his people and the Egyptians, giving advance warning about the plagues, e.g. hail, so that the Egyptians could avoid the consequences.

Visual Aids

Figures of Moses, Aaron and Pharaoh. Also make a window sheet using the cut-outs from the 3-5s activity (see diagram below). Place the cut-outs in the appropriate places on the backing paper, so that the windows can be folded back in turn to show each plague.

The older children can be asked which plague comes next prior to the windows being opened, and can then open the window to see if they are right. For the older classes, write the memory verse at the bottom. Hand this over to next week's teacher to use as a review before going on to the death of the firstborn.

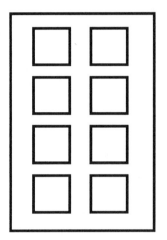

Activities / 3 - 5s

Photocopy pages 62 and 63 for each child. Prior to the lesson cut out the pictures from page 62 and place in an envelope for each child. The children glue the pictures in the appropriate places on page 63 and colour if time permits.

Activities / 5 - 7s

Photocopy pages 64 and the bottom part of this page for each child. Prior to the lesson cut out the pictures from this page and place in an envelope for each child. The children fill in the blanks on page 64 and then glue the pictures in the appropriate places. Check that the children know which plague is missing (darkness). Each child chooses one plague and draws it onto the picture of Pharaoh eating his dinner. Colour if time permits.

Activities / 7 - 9s

Make a plague wheel. Photocopy page 65 on card for each child. The children cut out both circles and cut out the marked segment on the top circle. Fill in the segments on the bottom circle as shown in the diagram.

Attach the circles together at X using a split pin paper fastener. The top circle can be revolved to show the different plagues. The children take it in turns to ask, 'Which plague is number ..... ?' When the other members of the group have answered the child asking the question checks the right answer by using the plague wheel.

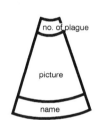

NOTE: A useful mnemonic for remembering the order of the plagues is:
Best football game for ages, but Hugh let Dick dribble.
(blood, frogs, gnats, flies, animal disease, boils, hail, locusts, darkness, death)

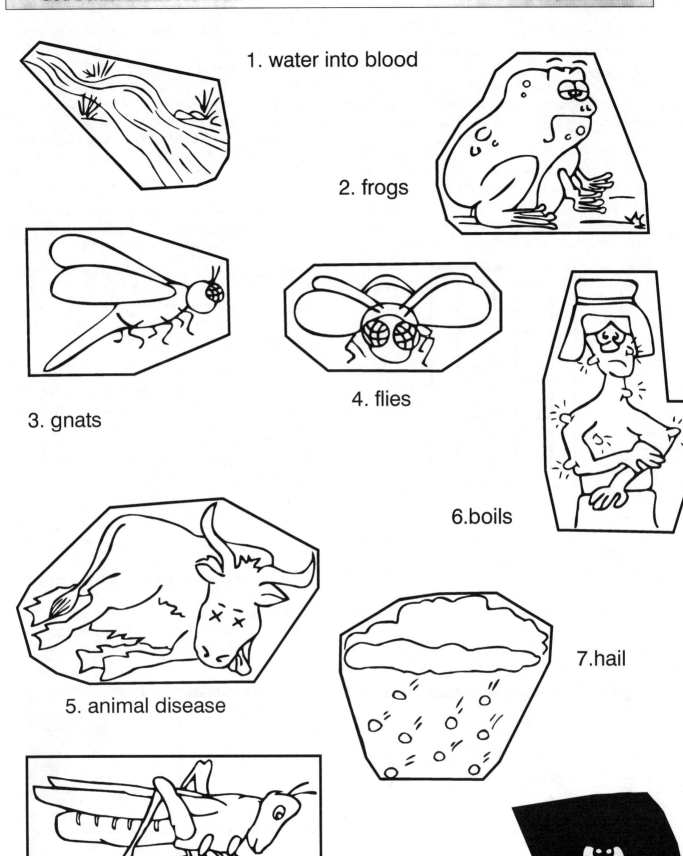

1. water into blood

2. frogs

3. gnats

4. flies

5. animal disease

6. boils

7. hail

8. locusts

9. darkness

The Plagues of Egypt Exodus 5:1 - 10:29

1. water into blood

2. frogs

3. gnats

4. flies

5. animal disease

6. boils

7. hail

8. locusts

9. darkness

In all things God works for good. Romans 8:28

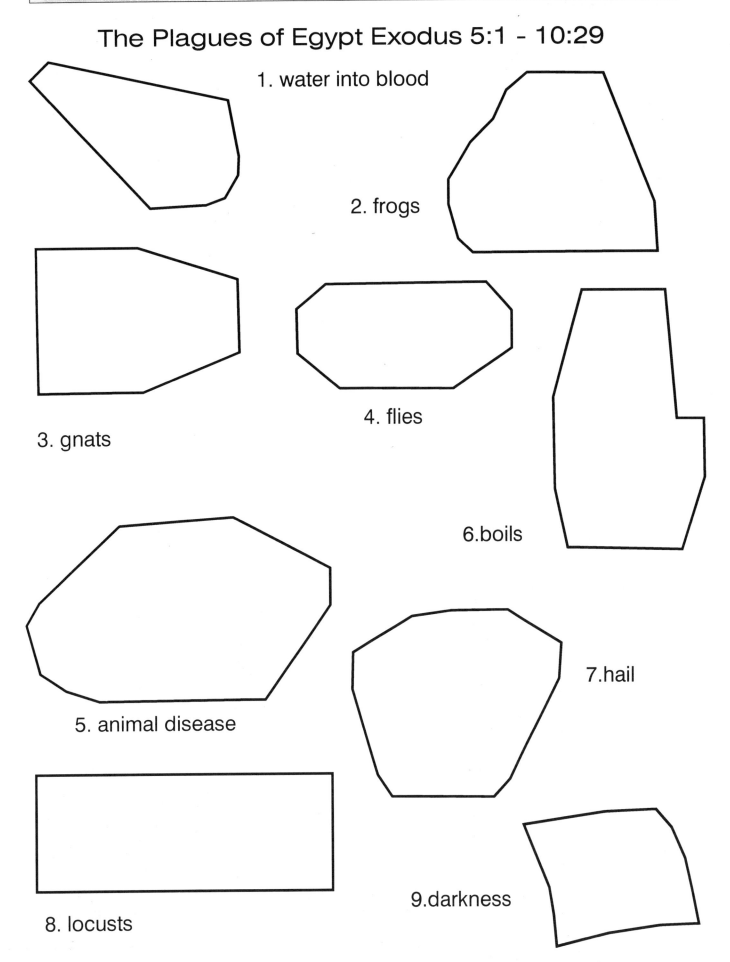

l _ c _ sts

?

_ ai l

?

_ oi _

?

on c _ tt _ e

?

_ lie _

the plagues

b _ oo _

?

_ r _ gs

?

gn _ t _

?

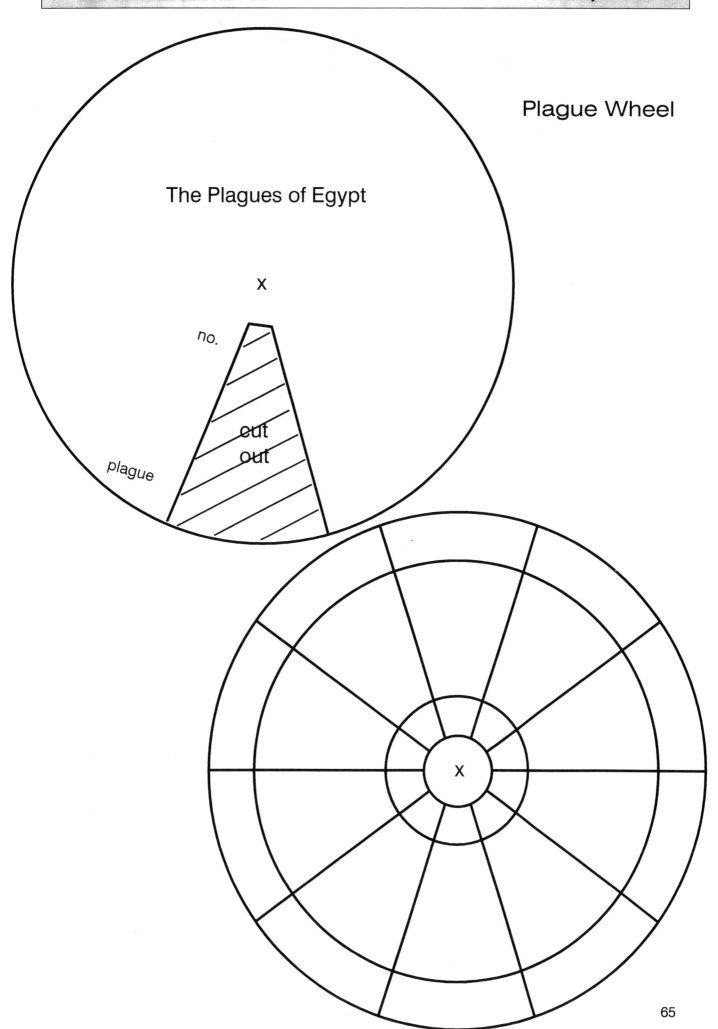

Plague Wheel

The Plagues of Egypt

x

no.

cut out

plague

x

WEEK 9
God Delivers His People

Preparation:
Read Exodus 11:1 - 12:42, using the Bible study notes to help you.

Lesson Aim:
To show how God saves his people from death and slavery in Egypt.

12:8	Bread baked without the yeast - i.e. baked in haste.
12:11	Shoes were not normally worn inside.
12:35-36	Cf. Exodus 3:21

During the months of the plagues Pharaoh had been given every opportunity to repent of his arrogance and acknowledge God, but had refused. This refusal caused judgment and distress to fall on the entire nation of Egypt.

Unlike the other plagues, when God used natural phenomena in supernatural ways, the death of the first-born was by direct intervention. Note that Moses and Aaron were not told to call up this plague - God stated the time and way he was to act.

In order to escape, the Israelites had to follow the specific instructions God gave to Moses. The older children can be shown how the Passover foreshadows Christ's death (John 1:29, 1 Corinthians 5:7) - the lamb had to be male, without defects, and its blood had to be shed and applied to the house; the people had to remain within the house if the blood was to be effective.

11:5	The firstborn of the cattle were esteemed and worshipped by the Egyptians.
12:2	Previously the Jewish year had begun in what is our September. From that time on it was to start in our mid-March. The Jewish religious year still starts at this point.

Lesson Plan

Recap on last week's lesson using the visual aid from last week. (Prior to the lesson draw a child on a bed behind window 10.) In today's true story from the Bible we will find out how God saved his people from Egypt. Ask the children to listen carefully so that they can tell you what instructions God gave his people to keep them safe.

At the end of the story go over the instructions the Israelites had to follow so that the angel of death would pass over them. Revise the memory verse. With the older children look back over the life of Moses, pointing out how God prepared Moses to be the saviour of his people. Compare the way God prepared Joseph to save his people from famine.

Visual Aids

The window sheet from last week.

Pictures of Israelite children and a door frame in which to place the children (see the activity for 7-9s). Red felt-tipped pen to mark the door posts and cross-beam at the appropriate point.

Photocopy pages 68, 69, and the bottom of this page on card for each child. Prior to the lesson cut out the house shape from page 68 and the house back from this page. Cut out the doorway (the hatched area), leaving the bottom step intact. Cut 2 slits where indicated. Cut out the slider from page 69.

Instructions

- Glue the side flaps of the house to the house back, then glue the top flap in place.

- Using a red crayon or felt tip pen, mark the top and the sides of the door with 'blood'.

- Colour the children on the slider. Insert the slider through the slits in the side of the house so that the children are visible in the doorway. 'Safe' is seen over the children's heads. Facing the house, pull the slider to the right so that the children appear at the side of the house. 'Not safe' can be seen over their heads.

- Use the activity to reinforce the lesson aim.

Follow the instructions on page 70.

Photocopy pages 72 and 73 back to back.

- Fold the page in half with the cross on the inside and the door on the outside.

- Cut around 3 sides of the door, leaving the left hand side intact. Fold the door outwards so that it can open and close. Insert a split pin paper fastener halfway down the right hand side of the door to act as a door knob.

- Colour the children on the inside of the door, the door and the cross. Mark the lintel and door posts with red to represent blood.

- Fold the card in half and glue the 2 halves together at the edges where indicated. The door can be opened to show the children on the inside of the door and the cross.

- Discuss with the children what 'Christ, our Passover lamb has been sacrificed' means and the need for personal application. Point out that just as the first born children could only be saved from death by the sacrifice of the lamb, so we have been saved from eternal death, (spending eternity without God), by Jesus' death on the cross. In order to benefit from the death of the lamb the children had to believe God's word and stay inside the house marked with the blood. In order for us to benefit from Jesus' death on the cross we must believe God's word - that Jesus is God and died in our place - and thank him for it.

top

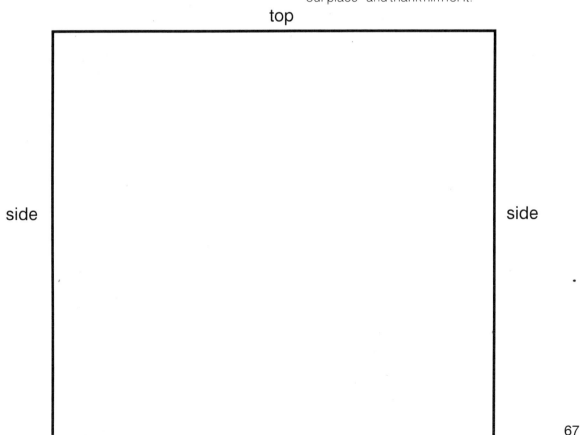

side   side

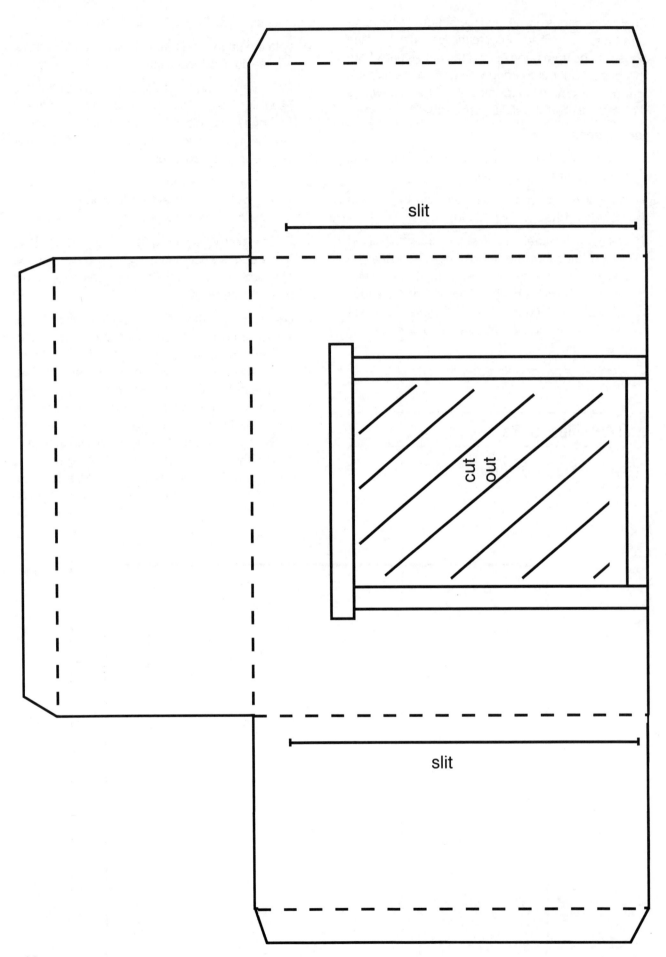

slit

cut out

slit

not

safe

Instructions
1. Photocopy pages 70 and 71 for each child.
2. The children draw lines to link the question with the pictures representing the correct answers.
3. Cut out the shapes from this page. This will give you pieces of a pyramid with your memory verse written on it. Build the pyramid, gluing it onto the bottom of page 71.

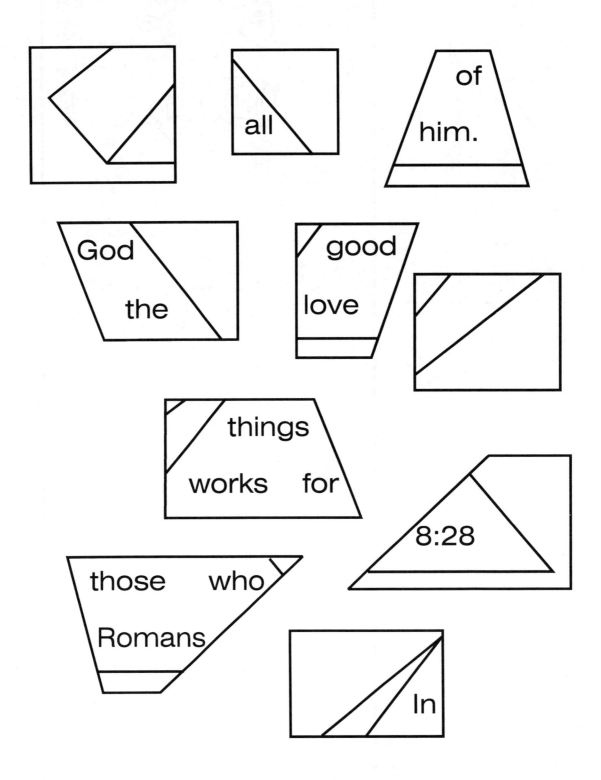

Who did God use to bring about his plans?

Pharaoh

Who knew they were doing God's will?

God was working for the good of ....

Children of Israel

Who did not know they were doing God's will?

Who was God going to give the Promised Land to?

Moses

Egyptians

Aaron

Can you think of a way in which God works for your good?

Build your pyramid here

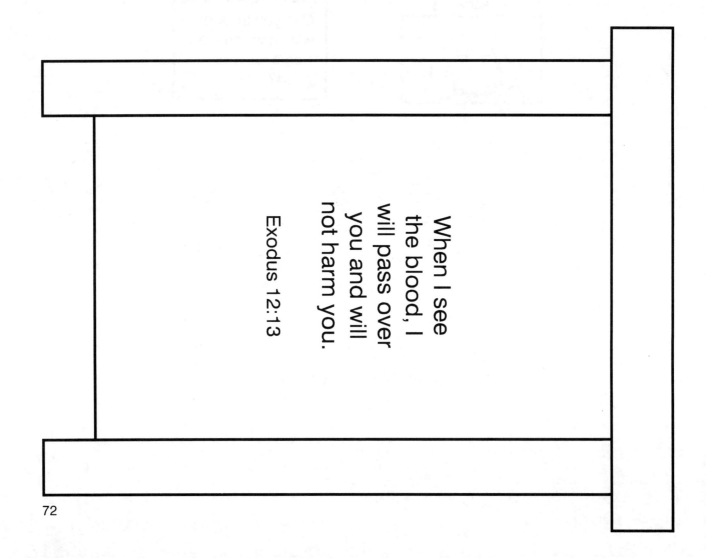

When I see
the blood, I
will pass over
you and will
not harm you.

Exodus 12:13

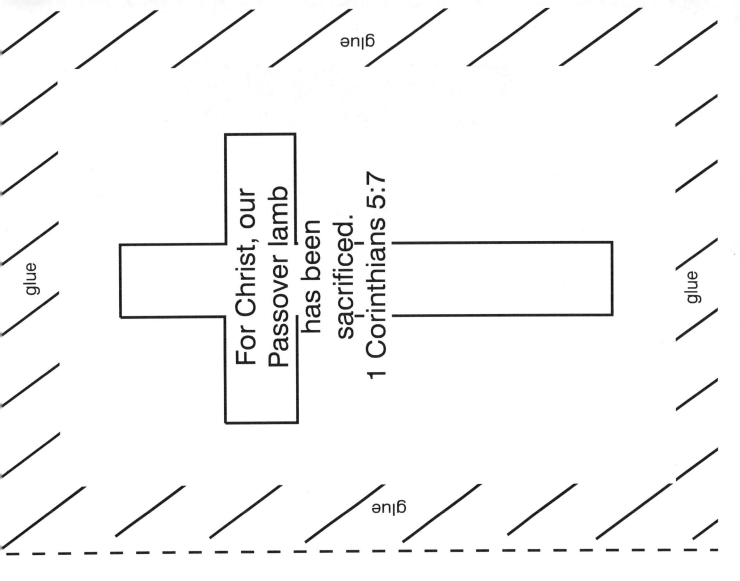

glue

For Christ, our Passover lamb has been sacrificed. 1 Corinthians 5:7

glue

glue

glue

Preparation:
Read Exodus 13:17 - 14:31, using the
Bible study notes to help you.

Lesson Aim:
To show how God saves his people from
destruction.

13:17-18	The direct way from Egypt to Canaan was along the coastal plain, but this was dominated by the Philistines. (See map on page 83).
13:19	Cf. Genesis 50:25.
14:1-2	God gives Moses specific instructions about the route, even though the pillars of cloud and fire were leading them. The proposed change appeared to lead them into a cul-de-sac. The Red Sea was to the east, and high mountains to the south and west; there was no way out, humanly speaking.
14:9	Pi-hahiroth was a range of impassable craggy rocks. Migdol and Baal Zephon were forts on the border of Egypt.
14:10-12	The Israelites' confidence in God is very short-lived (cf. Exodus 13:17), and they complain to Moses.
14:24	We are not told how God threw the Egyptians into a panic - just that he did so.

Lesson Plan

Show the children various things that help you find your way, e.g. a map, a compass, a light, a hooter, etc. Talk about going on a journey. What do we take with us? How do we know the way to go? Remind the children of last week's story. What did the Israelites take with them on their journey? How would they know which way to take to get to Canaan? In today's true story from the Bible we will find out how God showed his people the right way to go.

At the end of the story revise the memory verse and recap on how God had made all things work together for good in Moses' life.

Visual Aids

A map for the older children - see page 83.

Crossing the Red Sea

Requirements:

- roll of blue paper (paper must be of the type that will roll back if unrolled and let go suddenly).

- photocopy the Egyptians on page 76, and the Israelites on page 77. Cut out the Israelites and the Egyptians, colour and glue onto card so that they will stand up. Alternatively, use duplo or lego people.

Procedure:

1. Cut a length of blue paper to form a river. Roll up the remaining paper from both ends so they meet in the middle. Paint a section in the middle to look like the sea bed.

2. Prior to the lesson attach the river to a firm base, e.g. a table top. Attach the roll of paper to river so that the 'sea bed' is firmly anchored. Let the paper roll together in the centre.

3. Make a pillar of fire and a pillar of cloud from Smarties tubes covered with red paper and cotton wool.

4. During the story bring the crowd of Israelites to the edge of river. At the appropriate point unroll paper and anchor both ends with bluetak or drawing pins. The Israelites can walk across the river bed, chased by Egyptian soldiers. When the Israelites are safe on the other side of the river, but the Egyptians are still in the middle, release both

ends of the paper roll, which should then spring together, swallowing up the Egyptians.

Activities / 3 - 5s

Each child requires page 77 photocopied on white card, page 78 photocopied on green/sandy card, an A4 sheet of blue paper and cotton wool. Prior to the lesson cut off the pillar of cloud and cut out the children of Israel from page 77.

Instructions

- Colour the children of Israel.

- Roll the pillar of cloud into a tube and glue. Glue cotton wool round the top two thirds of the tube. Cut slits in the bottom of the pillar of cloud where marked. Bend the pieces outwards.

- Fold the sheet of blue paper in half widthways and cut along the fold. Using a pencil roll up each piece of blue paper tightly. When the pencil is pulled out of the middle the paper should stay in a loose roll.

- To assemble glue both halves of the river in place up to the dotted lines on page 78 (see diagram). Bend back the tab at the base of the children of Israel and glue to page 78. Glue the pillar of cloud where marked.

Activities / 5 - 7s

Each child requires page 79 photocopied on card, an A4 sheet of blue paper, 2 pieces of card measuring 21 x 3 cm., a stapler and glue.

Instructions

- Cut the sheet of blue paper in half widthways.

- Staple the 2 pieces of card to the halves of blue paper as shown (see diagram).

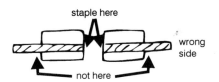

- Cut slots in page 79 where indicated. Colour the page if time permits.

- Insert the piece of card through the slot and glue the opposite edge of the blue paper to the edge of page 79 (see diagram).

- Pull the 2 pieces of card to see the sea roll back (see diagram).

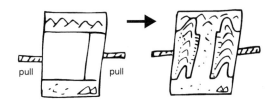

A revision game. Photocopy page 80 onto A3 paper and glue onto card to make a game board. Photocopy pages 81 and 82 onto card and cut out to make a pack of question cards. Follow the instructions on page 80. The game is suitable for a maximum of 6 players, so either provide one game for every 5/6 children or get the children to play in pairs.

cut ✂ _____

pillar of cloud

_____

_____

_____

_____

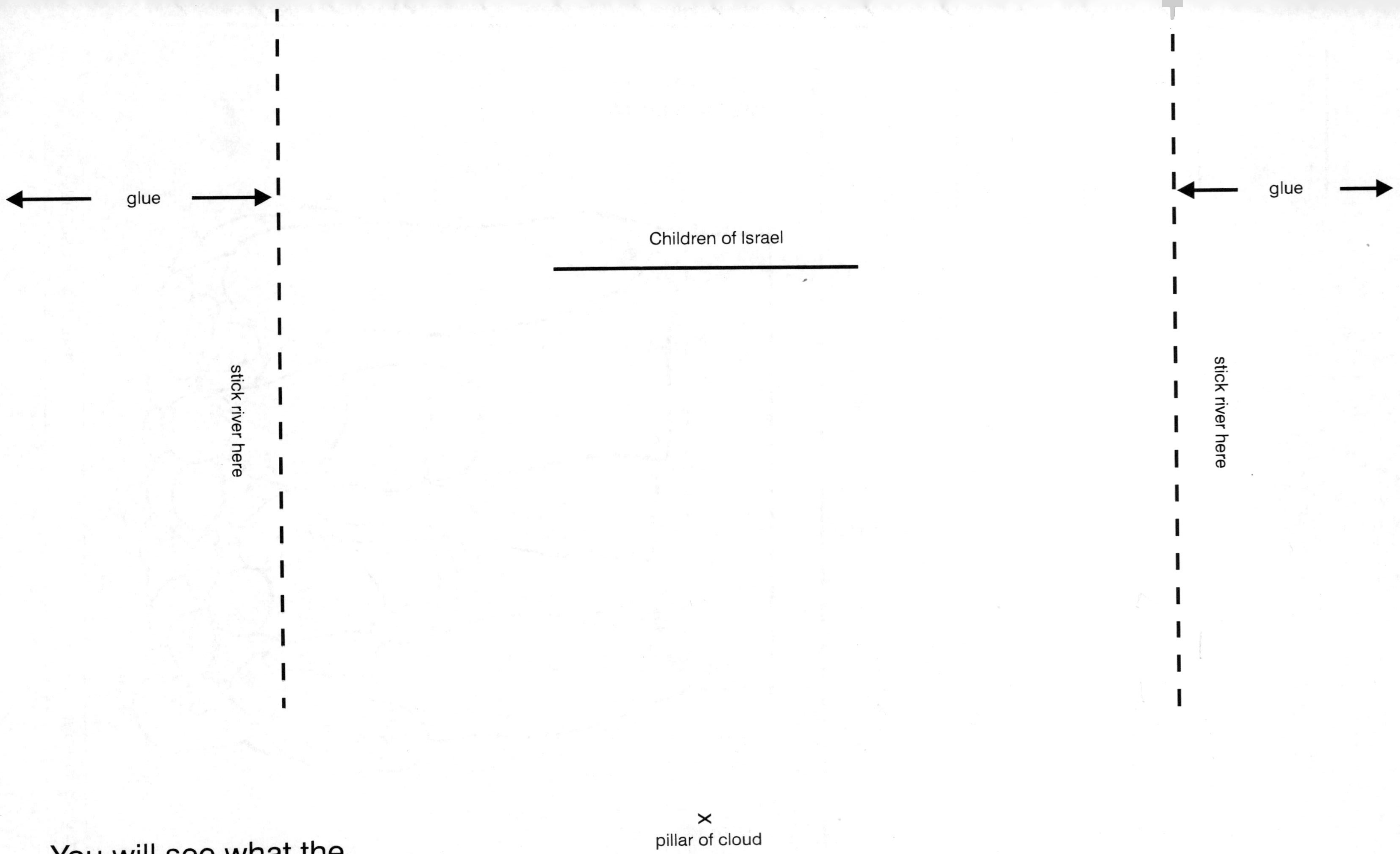

You will see what the
Lord will do to save you.

Exodus 14:13   78

X
pillar of cloud

glue

stick river here

Children of Israel

stick river here

glue

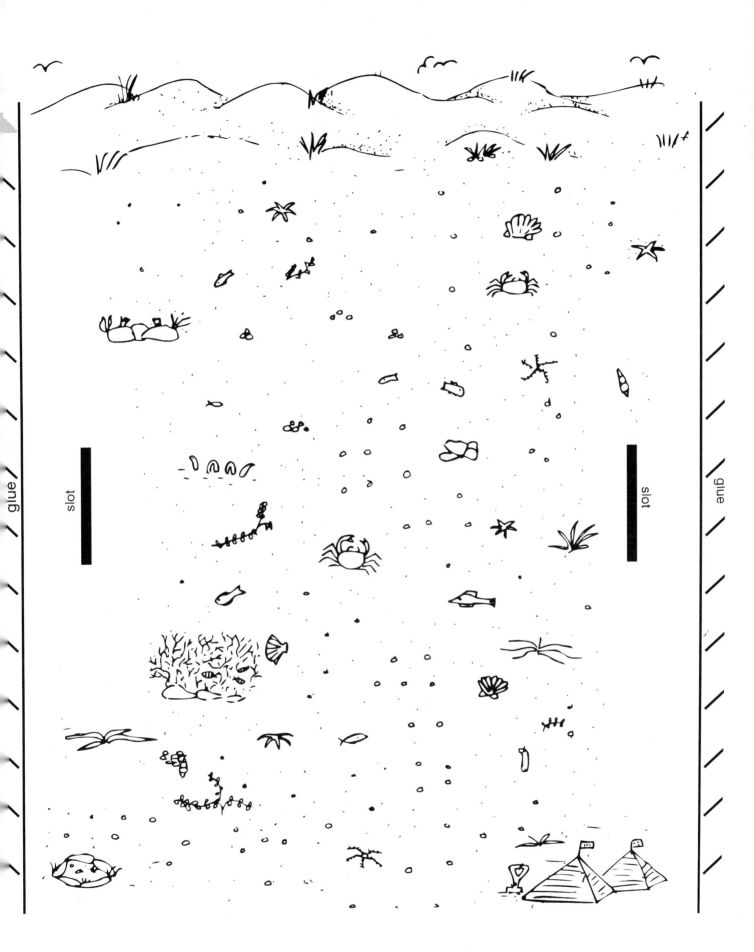

Requirements

A counter for each player

1 dice

1 pack of Question cards (shuffled).

Instructions

1. Throw the dice to decide who starts - the person who throws the highest number.

2. The play then moves in a clockwise direction.

3. Each player throws the dice and moves the number thrown. If he/she lands on a square with instructions written on it, these instructions must be obeyed. If he/she lands on a square with **Q** written on it, the leader takes the top question card and reads out the question.

   If the player answers correctly he/she moves forward 1 square.

   For an incorrect answer the player moves backwards 1 square.

4. The winner is the first player to reach square 49 **'Safe across the Red Sea'.**

NB for the teacher

This game is for revision of the Moses series. If an incorrect answer is given, see if any other player knows the answer. (A correct answer from another player does not result in that player's counter moving forward.)

The board (squares):

43	44	45	46	47	48	49
43	**Q**	45	**Q**	47	48 The people complain to Moses. Go back to square 32	49 **Safe across the Red Sea.**

42	41	40	39	38	37	36
42 **Q**	41	40 The Egyptians give the Israelites what they ask for. Go forward 1 square	39 Pharaoh drives the Israelites out of Egypt. Go forward 2 squares.	38	37 **Q**	36

29	30	31	32	33	34	35
29 **Q**	30	31 God makes a distinction between the Egyptians and the Israelites. Go forward 1 square	32	33 **Q**	34 **Q**	35 Pharaoh refuses to let the Israelites go. Go back 3 squares.

28	27	26	25	24	23	22
28	27 God performs miracles. Go forward 3 squares.	26 Pharaoh refuses to obey God. Miss 1 turn.	25	24 **Q**	23	22 Moses complains to God. Go back 3 squares.

15	16	17	18	19	20	21
15	16 **Q**	17	18 Pharaoh makes the Israelites work even harder. Go back to Egypt.	19	20 **Q**	21

14	13	12	11	10	9	8
14 God sends Aaron to be Moses' helper. Go forward 1 square	13	12 **Q**	11	10 **Q**	9	8 Moses objects to God's plan. Miss 1 turn.

1	2	3	4	5	6	7
1 **Egypt**	2	3 The Israelites become slaves. Go back 1 square.	4	5 **Q**	6 **Q**	7 Moses is rescued by Pharaoh's daughter. Go forward 2 squares.

Q. Why did Pharaoh make the Israelites his slaves?

A. There were so many of them that they were a threat to the Egyptians.

Q. Who did Miriam find to look after Moses for Pharaoh's daughter?

A. His mother.

Q. Who did God give Moses as a helper?

A. Aaron.

Q. What was the second plague?

A. Frogs.

Q. What was the fifth plague?

A. Animal (cattle) disease.

Q. What did Pharaoh tell the Egyptians to do to the Israelite babies?

A. Throw the boys into the river Nile.

Q. What was Moses doing when he saw the burning bush?

A. Looking after sheep.

Q. What punishment did Pharaoh give the Israelites when Moses asked him to let them go?

A. Make bricks without straw.

Q. What was the third plague?

A. Gnats.

Q. What was the sixth plague?

A. Boils.

Q. What did Moses' mother do when Moses was 3 months old?

A. Hid him in a basket at the water's edge.

Q. Give one of the excuses Moses made when God called him to lead the people out of Egypt?

A. I'm not good enough; I don't know who you are; they won't believe me; I can't speak clearly; I don't want to.

Q. What was the first plague?

A. Water into blood.

Q. What was the fourth plague?

A. Flies.

Q. What was the seventh plague?

A. Hail.

Q. What was the tenth plague?

A. Death of the first-born.

Q. What did God tell the Israelites to do to avoid the death of the first-born?

A. Kill a lamb, put the blood on the door posts, stay in the house.

Q. When they left Egypt why didn't God lead them by the shortest way?

A. He didn't want them to be afraid of the Philistines and turn back to Egypt.

Q. What did God tell Moses to do to make the waters divide?

A. Hold his stick over the sea.

Q. What is the memory verse?

A. In all things God works for the good of those who love him. Romans 8:28.

Q. What was the ninth plague?

A. Darkness.

Q. How did God show his graciousness to the Egyptians when he sent hail?

A. Either - warning not to go out **or** - sparing the wheat.

Q. What did the Egyptians give the Israelites before they left Egypt?

A. Whatever they asked for - silver and gold.

Q. How did God lead the Israelites by night?

A. A pillar of fire.

Q. What did God use to drive the sea back?

A. A strong, east wind.

Q. What was the eighth plague?

A. Locusts.

Q. What was the first plague **not** to effect the Israelites?

A. Flies

Q. What was special about the lamb chosen to be the Passover lamb?

A. No defects or blemishes.

Q. How did God lead the Israelites by day?

A. A pillar of cloud.

Q. Where was the pillar of cloud whilst the Israelites were crossing the Red Sea?

A. Between the Israelites and the Egyptians - who were behind the Israelites.

82

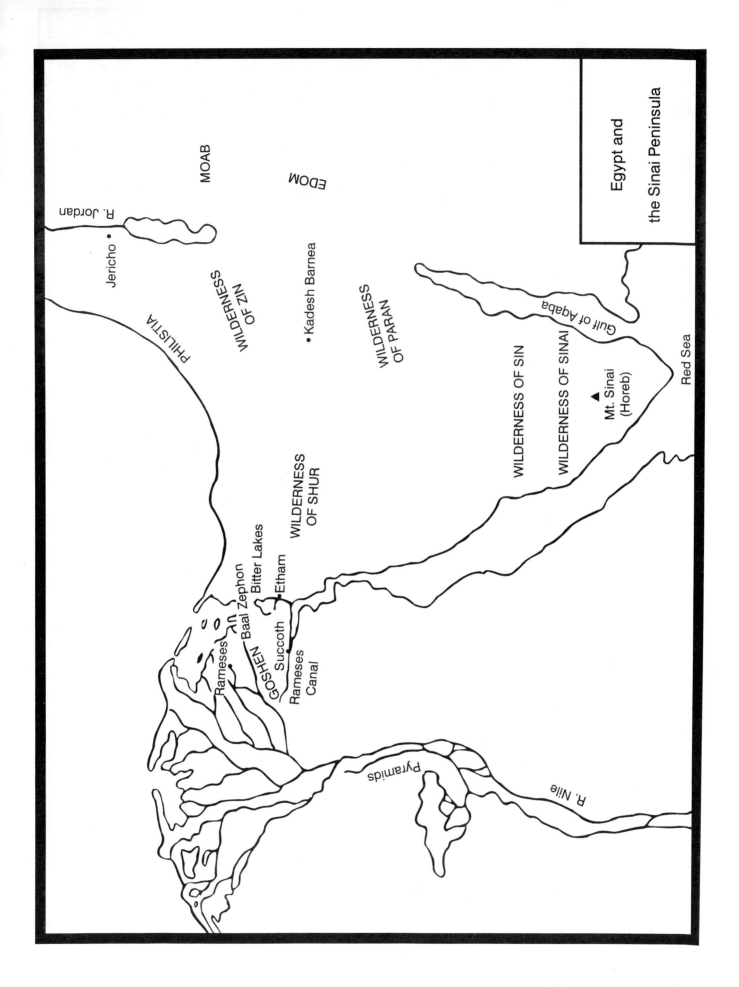

Egypt and
the Sinai Peninsula

MOAB

EDOM

R. Jordan

Jericho •

WILDERNESS
OF ZIN

• Kadesh Barnea

PHILISTIA

WILDERNESS
OF PARAN

Gulf of Aqaba

WILDERNESS OF SIN

WILDERNESS OF SINAI

▲ Mt. Sinai
(Horeb)

Red Sea

WILDERNESS
OF SHUR

Bitter Lakes

Baal Zephon

• Etham

Rameses

GOSHEN

Succoth

Rameses
Canal

Pyramids

R. Nile

Syllabus for On the Way for 3-9s

	Year 1	Year 2	Year 3
	Book 1 (13 weeks)	**Book 6 (10 weeks)**	**Book 11 (13 weeks)**
Old/New Testament	In the Beginning (3) Abraham (6) Jacob (4)	Samson (2) Ruth (2) Samuel (2) Saul (4)	Jesus Meets (3) God's Rules (10)
	Book 2 (12 weeks)	**Book 7 (13 weeks)**	**Book 12 (14 weeks)**
Christmas **New Testament**	Christmas Gifts (5) Jesus' Authority (7)	The Christmas Story (4) Preparation for Service (4) The Promised Messiah (5)	Heavenly Messengers (5) Jesus Helps (5) Parables of the Kingdom (4)
	Book 3 (13 weeks)	**Book 8 (9 weeks)**	**Book 13 (13 weeks)**
New Testament **Easter** **Early Church**	Prayer (4) Jesus is King (5) Peter (4)	Jesus Teaches (5) Parables of Judgment (2) The Easter Story (2)	Parables of the Vineyard (3) Jesus our Redeemer (3) The Early Church (3) Paul (4)
	Book 4 (10 weeks)	**Book 9 (10 weeks)**	**Book 14 (14 weeks)**
Old Testament	Joseph (4) Job (1) Moses (5)	David (7) Solomon (3)	Kings (5) Daniel (4) Esther (2) Nehemiah (3)
	Book 5 (10 weeks)	**Book 10 (11 weeks)**	
Old Testament	In the Wilderness (4) Joshua (4) Gideon (2)	Elijah (5) Elisha (4) Jonah (2)	

The books can be used in any order; the above plan is the suggested order.
The syllabus is chronological; Christmas to Easter is all about Jesus, followed by 3 series on the early church (1 in Book 3 and 2 in Book 13). The rest of each year consists of lessons from the Old Testament. Old Testament and New Testament lessons are in separate books (apart from Book 11), so the books can be used in whatever order is required. The books contain differing numbers of lessons, so that they fit the required number of weeks between Christmas and Easter and the following Christmas.
The number in brackets indicates the number of lessons in a series.

For more information about *On The Way for 3-9s* please contact:
Christian Focus Publications, Geanies House, Fearn, Tain, Ross shire, IV20 1TW / Tel: (01862) 871 011 or
TnT Ministries, 29 Buxton Gardens, Acton, London, W3 9LE / Tel: (0181) 992 0450

Teacher's Challenge Solution

  pages 26, 43, 75.